Death, Too, For The-Heavy-Runner

Ben Bennett

Illustrations by Tom Saubert

MOUNTAIN PRESS PUBLISHING COMPANY

Missoula, Montana

1981

Library of Congress Cataloging in Publication Data

Bennett, Ben.
  Death, too, for The-Heavy-Runner.

  Bibliography: p.
1. Siksika Indians — History.   2.   Heavy Runner,
Blackfeet Chief. I.   Title.
E99.S54B46   970.004'97   80-15903
ISBN 0-87842-131-9
ISBN 0-87842-132-7 (pbk.)
Second printing, 1984

Introduction

A YEAR'S RESEARCH at the Montana Historical Society, Blackfeet Agency, Museum of the Plains Indian, and National Archives went into this account of the Marias River massacre of January 23, 1870.

To the best of my ability, it is accurate, objective, and complete. To the best of my knowledge, it is also verifiable, with these exceptions:

While true to Blackfeet cultural traditions, the visions of Mountain-Chief and The-Heavy-Runner are products of imagination.

So, to a far lesser extent, are the visions of Generals Sully, Sheridan, and deTrobriand, which, while factually supportable, reflect my own conclusions as well.

The content of Alfred Sully's meeting with The-Heavy-Runner and other chiefs on January 1, 1870, can be confirmed, but the actual dialogue is fictional, as are the words of The-Heavy-Runner at the time of Major Baker's attack.

The accounts of the massacre attributed to Black-Antelope and Bear-Head are in part quoted and in remainder adapted from James Willard Schultz's *Blackfeet and Buffalo,* published in 1962 by the University of Oklahoma Press, which gave permission for their use, and to which acknowledgment and thanks are due.

Finally, the Horace Clarke and Joseph Kipp statements regarding the massacre were, in fact, taken many years later, in support of a claim against the government by descendants of The-Heavy Runner. There is no reason to believe, however, that their contemporary accounts would have differed in any significant respect, or to doubt that those accounts were known to General deTrobriand.

Ben Bennett
San Francisco
March 1981

For my grandfather, George Eugene Everingham; my great aunt, Alice Ballard Hanchett; and my good friend, Doris Mary Greenwald Milton.

Acknowledgments

Harriett Meloy, Brian Cockhill, and John Mason of the Montana Historical Society Library helped make the research a pleasure, as did Ramon Gonyea of the Museum of the Plains Indian. I thank them. Alice Davies and my sister, Elise Heuser, read the manuscript with insight and objectivity. I thank them also. Edward Darling encouraged and supported me. He is now dead, and I think of him often.

Table of Contents

The Blackfeet Nation

The Blackfeet Nation consists of three tribes: the Pikuni or Piegans, the Kainah or Bloods, and the Siksika or Blackfeet. Many years ago the Blackfeet ranged from north of Edmonton, Alberta, to the Yellowstone River. They were quick to resent and avenge insult or wrong, but powerful and loyal allies when their friendship was won. They were greatly feared by early trappers and settlers because of the vigor with which they defended their hereditary hunting grounds from encroachment. No tribe ever exceeded them in bravery.

Historical Marker
Entering Blackfeet Reservation
Browning, Montana

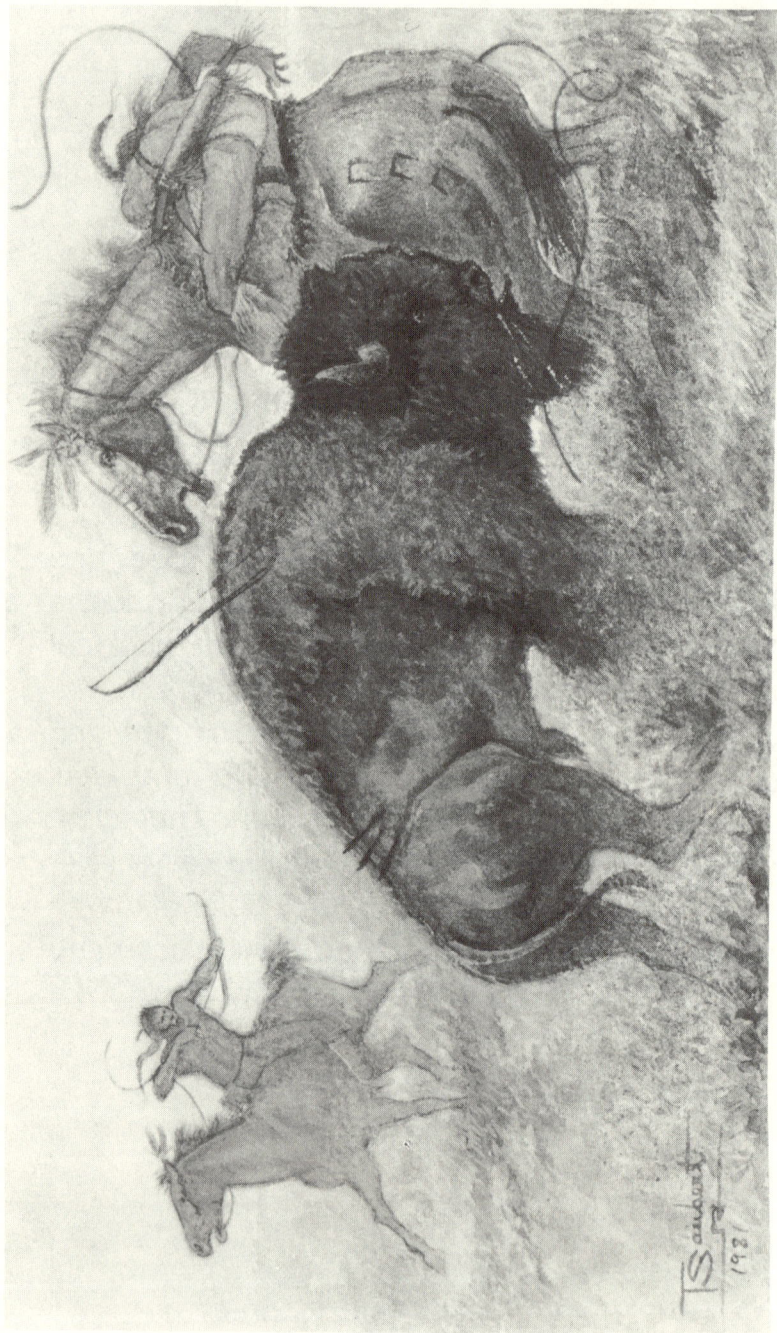

The horse man closed...

The Ancient Blackfeet
Pre-history to 1830

Eastern FROM the Rocky Mountains extends that area of the northern plains known as the short grass prairie. Baked by suns and buried by snows, parched by drought and drenched by downpour, this broad platter of tan earth knows well the harshness of life's hand. Its sandy soil holds little water and erodes easily. Rocky outcroppings, table-topped buttes, and deep, jagged gorges afford the only relief from its vast expanse of flatlands. The muted browns and grays of its bunchgrass, prickly pear, wormwood, and sage are brightened only for a few wet weeks in spring, and by the cottonwoods which crowd the banks and bottoms of its creeks and rivers. It is a dry, dun-colored land, made drier still by the west winds that sweep and shape it, imperceptibly, irresistibly, without pity or pause.

Captain Meriweather Lewis called it The Great Northern Desert. The Blackfeet named it Ground-Of-Many-Gifts.

To the west, the Rockies stand, a dark and mysterious presence beyond the flatlands and the finite minds of men. The Blackfeet called them Backbone-Of-The-World, and feared them.

The Backbone is no place for the Blackfeet, they said. Its gods are not our gods, and they do strange and cruel things to us plains people when they get the chance. We must make strong medicine to escape them.

From the Backbone came Wind-Maker in the shape of a giant bull elk, his ears flapping; and Cold-Maker, chief of the Always-Winter-Land, shooting blizzards from his bow. From the Backbone came Thunder, the great bird who flies with clouds and fires lightning from his eyes; and spirits of the restless dead riding the wings of owls.

The Blackfeet saw the Backbone as remote and sinister, but they also knew its gentler side. It sent Snow-Shrinker, the black chinook wind of winter, howling heavy in the night from arching clouds, bringing warmth from the All-Over-Water to a frozen land. And from the Backbone flowed the numberless streams that brought life itself to the land, streams the white man named Dearborn and St. Mary's, Armell and Timber. The Blackfeet knew them as Shield-Floated-Away and Many-Chiefs-Gathered, It-Crushed-Them and Big-Raven-Went-Crazy-Here, and knew they fed not a barren wasteland but a fertile ocean of rich, short grass. Under blades only inches high, its roots burrowed deep beneath the dry, dusty surface and clung to the nourishment below. It might be brown and seem withered, but within its tough dry stalks flowed life, life in overwhelming abundance, life bursting from beneath a mask of death.

And as the ground nourished grass, sweet timothy and wiry grama, so the grass supported grazing. Given life, it in turn gave life to the four-foots, to Prairie-Trotter and Wagging-Tail, Black-Disappearing, Striped-Face, and Sticky-Mouth. And homes, to flocks of wild turkeys and prairie chickens, to jackrabbits, long-eared explosions of energy, and to prairie dogs by the twitching millions in their labyrinthine civilizations — every bird and animal at home in its own territory, whether in high lands or low.

2

But most of all, it gave life and home to the buffalo. Unimaginable herds of buffalo, herds one hundred miles across and more, larger than any herds of any animals ever seen before or since upon the face of the earth. Buffalo countless as stars, horizon to horizon, huge of head and hump, on legs slender as antelopes', darkened the plains. Dull beasts standing motionless, only dimly discerning the threatened predations of wolf or man, or startled into day-long, sheep-like flight without apparent cause. Dull, small-minded beasts to whom the Blackfeet were bound by sinews of survival. Without buffalo there would be no food, no clothing, no lodge covers; without buffalo, no life.

It had not always been so. When Napi, the Old-Man, made the world and its creatures, he gave his Black-Footed-People not a prairie but a forest land to live in, dogs to help move camp, and the knowledge that they would not live forever and so should feel sorry for one another. For centuries they lived in such a place and way, until another people, a people light-skinned and pos-sessed of many wonders, arrived from across the All-Over-Water. Nearly two centuries passed before the Blackfeet saw one of these strange people face to face, but from the tales of his powers they knew he was especially favored and they called him Napikwan, Old-Man's-Peo-ple. And they felt his powers also, as he displaced tribes from the east, crowding them into the western woodland and forcing the Blackfeet farther and farther west until they reached the Backbone. There they would go no farther. There, in the shadow of that jagged ridge of ice and rock scraping the sky, on the rim of the world, they built their lodges and their lives.

And there they first met the buffalo and learned his ways.

When Napi made the world, men were without

3

weapons, helpless against the ferocious buffalo that pursued and killed them and ate their flesh. So Napi taught his Black-Footed-People to make bows and arrows, and to drive the buffalo herds over cliffs. Man became the hunter and buffalo the hunted. Man learned to stalk the buffalo — alone and on foot, hidden beneath the skin of Big-Mouth, the prairie wolf, brother to his camp dogs. He learned to hunt with others of his band, surrounding small herds on the plains. From the winter shelter of woods and valleys to the summer feeding grounds in open country he followed the buffalo, observing his seasons. When yellow flowers of the tooth grass bloomed during early summer's Moon-When-Strawberries-Ripen, the stringy, muscular meat of bulls became tender and sweet, and he ate it spiced with the onion-like camas root, dug by his woman during Thunder-Moon. Buffalo hair shortened during mid-summer moons, making lighter the task of preparing lodge covers. In autumn's Moon-When-Snakes-Go-Blind, cows reached their prime, and the camps were red with raw meat and rich with the mixture of meat and chokecherries called pemmican, stored in rawhide parfleches against the winter moons, when the long-haired hides were warmest for robes. And when the geese returned and the New-Grass-Moon rose, experienced warriors passed on to their sons the secrets of the hunt to be proved on new-born calves.

Many were the seasons of the buffalo, and as many his bounties. From the gristle of his nose, sucked by the toothless ones of infancy and old age, to his tufted tail, used as he had used it to brush flies away, the buffalo was for the Blackfeet a four-legged larder, a warehouse of the wild. They ate him entire, tongue and testicles, brains and blood, muscle and marrow. They ate him raw, fresh as he fell, or roasted his great boss ribs over open fires. In long thin strips they dried his flesh in the sun. From his hide they fashioned lodge covers, containers for food and water, clothing from winter caps to moccasins. His hair they braided into rope, his sinews supplied bow strings and thread. From his horns came cups and ladles, from his hooves rattles. From his gallstones they extracted yellow pigment, from his bones they crafted tools and toys. Far from firewood, they burned his dung for fuel. He was Napi's gift to the Black-Footed-People that they might live, his greatest gift on the Ground-Of-Many-Gifts.

But the gift was more than the sustenance and support of their bodies, for the ways of the buffalo also shaped the minds and hearts of the Blackfeet - he taught them the oneness of life, and the kinship of life's children.

Napi despises wasters of life, the Blackfeet said. He made the buffalo for our use, but we may not kill more than we need, for he is our brother.

He supplied all needs, and so taught the Blackfeet to live contained and complete within the circle of the land and its life. From him they learned to be generous, as Napi's hand had opened to them, and to live as a community, sharing equally the rigors of the hunt and its rewards.

So lived the Blackfeet at the dawn of the eighteenth century, one nation among many such nomadic nations, their footsteps following the trails of the buffalo across the northern plains, living as all such people must within the delicate, demanding harmonies of a kind and cruel earth. And so they lived until, in a winking of Napi's eye, life ended and began anew. A strange sound echoed its passing, the different drumming of a distant hoofbeat heralded its birth. Its first faint rhythm pounded over the prairies to a band of Blackfeet stalking buffalo. Louder it grew, and they more alert and wondering, until before them ranged a war party of the Snake-People, not on foot, face to face in classic confrontation, but from astride huge, fleet animals the Blackfeet had never before seen. They called them Elk-Dogs, and knew that unless they too rode these fabulous beasts, their enemies would soon overwhelm them.

In his wisdom, Napi gave all that lived a way in the world. To some he gave flight, to others the fleetness of prairie fire; eyes that see far he gave, and ears that catch the faintest footfall. To man he gave mind and hand. There was a sure and simple purity in his plan. Birds soared and flew. Beasts stalked and ran. Men wondered and worked. Life afoot was man-sized, low to the ground, paced by the stride of man and scaled to his vision, circling with his seasons. Now it would surge and quicken, swell and expand to the powers of a new being, larger than life, faster and stronger and more cunning than any ever imagined by Old-Man. The day of the Horse-Man had dawned.

From friendly tribes to the west the Blackfeet purchased Elk-Dogs and learned the first tentative skills of horsemanship. They returned to their lodges beneath the Backbone confident and proud, taller than Blackfeet had ever been, certain that the Snakes could now be driven forever from the Ground-Of-Many-Gifts.

But Blackfeet hunting grounds would in many other ways never again be the same, for a volcano of change now erupted over the plains, an upheaval staggering in its impact, sweeping before it all the old ways.

Gone was the old hunt. Afoot it had been a parody of pursuit, a trial of patience and endurance, the kill an instant of naked peril, when fear and courage tore a man apart. Now only coyotes crawled, only wolves feared the flailing hooves and horns. The Horse-Man chased! A headlong chase after glory, a carefree game, a breathless dash into the face of the wind, faster than Wind-Maker, howling with the thunder of the chase.

Let the bull see! Let him hear! Let him know the Horse-Man comes! Let him run until his eyes rain blood and his tongue drags in the dust! Let him race until his heart bursts! Let him roar in fury and terror! He cannot escape the Horse-Man!

And the Horse-Man's prize was a horn of plenty, spilling out the promise of camps never cold, of parfleches forever full.

Gone, too, were the old ways of war. Afoot, the Blackfeet had fought to survive, protecting old hunting grounds or carving out new ones. Great numbers took the field, often for many days and after long marches, for the right to hunt and the right to live were one, worth dying to defend. But now passed the age of the plodding pawn, rooted in place, of shield facing enemy shield. A new day dawned — the day of the Horse-Man, fire-eyed raider of the plains. His belly full, he felt a new hunger. Certain of survival, now he could live.

Let the old ones tell their tales of long-ago days. Let the timid tend their lodgefires. Tonight, far from their fires, the raiders enter the camp of the Crows, naked bodies rubbed with sap of the cottonwood to conceal the man-smell. Close by the lodges, rustling at the limits of their tethers, stand the ponies most prized by warriors: tireless buffalo runners and war horses, lovers of the chase and kill. Tomorrow they belong to the Blackfeet. And should the Crows waken, take courage! Howl to the night skies the songs of war! All Crows are dogs! They tremble at the sight of Blackfeet medicine! Far better to die as Blackfeet than to live as Crows!

And if the raid were favored and the raiders fortunate, many coups would be counted, many horses captured, and new voices heard in the councils. For in the age of plenty, not the hunter but the raider ruled. Cunning and courage were his resources, power and position his rewards.

The Horse-Man saw not just a new world around him, but new worlds beyond his sight as well.

In the beginning, Napi walked his world to see that it was good. Hills and prairies he walked, forests and marshes, living with his children as one of them, to know their ways and their rightness. Satisfied that all lived well, the World-Maker slept.

But the world of the Horse-Man was grander than Napi's vision, and while Old-Man slept, another awoke. From a far-off lodge in the All-Over-Water rose not a strider of earth but the rider of skies, a maker not of worlds but of days, not of life but of light — the Sky-Chief, Sun.

With all their brothers of all the tribes, all the Lone People of the plains, the Blackfeet turned from the earthbound divinities of forest days to the worship of this new god whose eyes each day both beheld and illuminated the great circle of the universe.

Over all the Sky-Chief rode, source of all power, all in his sight of-the-sun, sacred and sun-favored. And over all he ruled, over the world without, the world of sap and substance, and over the world within, the spirit world. There dwelt the Above-Persons, Ground-Persons, and Underwater-Persons, spirits who had not Sun's power but were strongly of it, spirits who, if they chose, could help a man find favor in Sun's sight. For as a man's eyes were blinded if he gazed into the face of Sun, so his prayers could not penetrate directly to Sun's soul, source of all energy and power, but required an intercessor, the secret helper Blackfeet called Nitsokan, the dream. Nitsokan came from the child of Sun and his mate, Night-Light, the moon, the child named Early-Riser, the morning star, the bringer of dreams. In the shape of beaver the Wood-Biter

8

the dream appeared, or of otter the Killer-Of-Fish. As bear or buffalo it came, or as raven, who sees far, or wolf, who is never hungry. To each person, individual and alone, the dream came with the promise of protection and aid, of victory in war and success in the hunt, of good health and long life, of participation in the power of Sun.

This you must do, Nitsokan told the dreamer, showing him how to paint his lodge, his clothing, and his body. These songs sing to me, the dream commanded, and these prayers make. Wag your head in these dances, offer these gifts, and smoke these pipes. All this do as I have shown you, and I will be your secret helper. My powers you, and you alone, will have, to live in Sun's favor.

And in that favor, uniquely his, in that special relationship set forth by Nitsokan, each man lived alone with Sky-Chief, each lodge a pyramid to the Bringer-Of-Days, who each dawn made the light and recreated Napi's world.

Only at the great summer tribal encampment did the Blackfeet Horse-Men gather as one to honor Sky-Chief, building the sacred lodge that bore his name and symbolized his power. Only there as one they fulfilled their vows and recounted their coups, danced the ritual dances, and sang the ritual songs. And only there as one they celebrated with the medicine woman and her priests of Sun the opening of the turnip bundle, recalling once again the bride of Early-Riser who first brought to Blackfeet the secrets of Sun. Only then stood the Horse-Man other than alone, hand-in-hand with his secret helper and the maker of his days.

From the buffalo the Blackfeet learned the meaning of community and the oneness of life, to be sufficient unto the land and generous with its gifts. From the horse they learned the joys of self. As hunter and warrior, as child of

9

the universe and priest in its service, the new Horse-Man discovered himself as individual. More than a member of his band and tribe, more than mere clansman or cell of the communal body, he stood now unique, a product not just of tribal life but of his own energy and daring. Let others do as they would or must, his quest was his alone, and his alone its pleasure and its pain. His alone to know the thrill of the chase, to feel his man-beast body charged with its lightning or crushed by its thunder. His alone to know the dark night-secrets of the raid, to feel its fierce joys or bitter agonies. His alone to know the bounty of Sun's favor or the wretchedness of his curse. The Horse-Man lived beyond the boundaries of Napi's world, unfettered by its limits and deeper than its core. To the horizon of his own imagination, there stretched the vastness of the Horse-Man's land and life. To the endurance of his new legs, now doubled, as on wings he flew, in company when he sought it, alone as he chose — a free man and joyful, joyful and free — a gifted one on the Ground-Of-Many-Gifts.

In such spirit the generations of Blackfeet Horse-Men lived on the northern plains, testing and proving their powers and their pride, building an empire on and of the short sweet grass, an Indian nation unsurpassed by any in size and strength, and equalled only by the confederacies of Sioux, Cheyenne, and Arapaho on the central plains, and of Comanche, Kiowa, and Apache on the southern. Before them they drove Snake and Kutenai, Assiniboin, Crow, and Cree, carving out a nation larger by twice than New England, a nation rich in buffalo and beaver, over which they rode and ruled as warriors and as kings, speaking no other's language, for their own rich and complex tongue was best, as were all their ways. None entered or traversed the nation but in peril, for the Blackfeet were zealous warriors and jealous kings, fierce in their guardian-ship of the land and its gifts.

Three hundred centuries, ten times three thousand years, had passed since Stone Age ancestors of the Black-feet crossed a bridge of glacial ice from Asia in pursuit of giant bearlike game. A planet had warmed. Continents and seas had formed and filled, entire species had evolved and been extinguished. Races of men had flourished and fallen, their societies and civilizations, congresses and countries ascending in brilliance, collapsing into ashes and sand. Timed to the infinite sweep of the cosmic clock, seemingly timeless, shaped like a shoreline to the ageless rhythm of tide and wave, cycling with the galaxies, earth had given birth to her living and buried her dead. And through thirty thousand years the Black-Footed-People and their fathers had paced their lives to hers.

It would not be so for long. The chronicle of centuries was dwindling to days. Brothers to the west wind, the Blackfeet now rode the hurricane.

The world which had endured from the beginning of time, the way of life which Napi had created for his Black-Footed-People over thousands of generations, would in but a few turns lie buried beneath the trading posts of the light-skinned Napikwan and his treaties, beneath his boundaries, his baptisms, and his bullets.

The proper treatment of the original occupants of this land — the Indians — is one deserving of care and study. I will favor any course towards them which tends to their civilization, Christianization, and ultimate citizenship.

Ulysses S. Grant
First Inaugural Address
March 4, 1869

Fort Benton stood at the doorway.

Grant's Peace Policy
March 4 to July 16, 1869

ULYSSES S. GRANT favored the "civilization, Christianization, and ultimate citizenship" of the American Indian, and in the days following his inauguration as eighteenth president of the United States, he made clear what that meant:

All Indians would be moved off open hunting grounds and on to reservations.

Christian schools and churches would be established for their intellectual and spiritual uplifting.

No more Indian treaties would be negotiated, thereby ending the "fiction of tribal sovereignty" and confirming that the Indian was and would continue to be a ward of the government.

The government would no longer deal with chiefs or other tribal leaders, but would work toward equal status and universal citizenship for all Indians.

Grant was certain the plan would work; so certain in fact, that just three days after the inauguration he directed his Civil War comrade and friend General Philip Henry Sheridan to make the announcement a nation weary of conflict had been praying for:

"The Indian wars," said Sheridan, "are over."

The winter campaign just past, he explained, culminating in the battle of Washita River with the defeat of the

15

Cheyenne and the death of their chief Black Kettle, had persuaded all Indians that further resistance was useless. They would now proceed to the reservations assigned, prepared to give up the path of war and travel the white man's road.

The date was March 7, 1869, seven years before Little Big Horn and twenty until Wounded Knee.

The Eastern press labeled Grant's proposals the "Peace Policy," and called them good. But the Montana frontier disagreed.

On March 19, the Montana *Post* reported the season's first Indian disturbance, a Sioux raid along the Yellowstone River in which two whites were said to have been murdered.

On April 2, the *Post* wrote of Blackfeet having stolen twenty-one horses; on April 9, reported the murder of a soldier (known to be a victim of Indians because $350 was left on his person) and the chasing of a wagon by a band of Bloods and Piegans; and on April 16, carried rumors of three men having been killed and an undetermined number wounded by Blackfeet at White's Gulch.

"The winter being over and the necessity for being good and virtuous Indians having ceased to urge them forward in the paths of rectitude," editorialized the *Post*, "they have assumed the hardihood to insult the dignity of the Great White Father." Concluded the paper ominously: "Danger is not imminent, but disaster is at all times possible."

Events soon convinced the *Post* of the wisdom of its warning.

On May 28, it presented in grisly detail an account of an Indian raid along the Musselshell River in which a white woman had been scalped. Ten Indians were killed in the attack, and as a deterrent to others, their severed heads

16

were placed on public display with suitable inscriptions. ("Men rendered desperate by such provocations are not likely to stand on nice points of postmorten etiquette," commented the newspaper.)

With that incident, the *Post* had seen enough of both war parties and peace policies.

"When will our Indian policy be changed?" it asked on June 4. "How long, how long will the blood of innocent murdered men cry out against a policy more cowardly and disgraceful than ever dishonored a nation, ancient or modern? How long will the butchery of good citizens by these bloody fiends invoke the curses of western people upon a government that wantonly fails to protect its citizens from a savage foe?"

Far from being at an end, wrote the *Post,* the Indian wars would "endure for years and years," explaining:

"The causes of war will continue while the larger game lasts, unless sooner the Indians learn their inferiority and submit to their destinies."

As for "this reservation business," it added, it "can never be a success until the tribes are...reduced to a mere handful of decrepit and diseased creatures each."

"All evil must end," insisted the *Post.*

It was time to get on with the crusade.

*   *   *

Earlier in the spring of 1869, the government agency for the Blackfeet had been moved from Fort Benton on the Missouri to a new site on the Teton River — not so much because the new location was so good as because the old one had become so bad.

"The whiskey trade is carried on at Benton to a fearful extent," the Blackfeet agent had written in January. "The

Bloods are on a continual spree. The Piegans are afraid that the whiskey trade will bring on war with the whites. I fear the consequences."

And well he might, for by the early summer of 1869, Fort Benton was spoiling for a fight.

Only three years before, celebrating the twentieth anniversary of its founding as an American Fur Company post, Fort Benton had basked contentedly in a reality of frontier affluence and a vision of still greater prosperity to come. Although the once-dominant fur trade had passed its prime, the discovery of gold in Montana Territory had more than replaced the fur trade in luring fortune-seekers to the northern plains, and Fort Benton stood at the doorway. From whatever direction they came, it was at Fort Benton they entered; whatever their destination, it was from Fort Benton they left, for the tiny town marked the intersection of all the great highways, land and water, of the Northwest. On the Missouri River, wide and shallow, smooth and slow, winding twelve hundred miles east and south to St. Louis and civilization, Fort Benton was the last stop. Via six hundred mountainous miles of the Mullan Road, Benton connected with Fort Walla Walla at the head of navigation on the Columbia, tumbling westward to the sea. South to Helena and beyond, north to the Hudson Bay Company forts and farther, all trails spun out and away from Fort Benton.

"The Chicago of the West," her boosters called her, and grew rich backing up the boast.

Brown and ugly the Missouri might be ("too thick to drink and too thin to plant"), and rough and rutted those frontier trails, but to Bentonites they were rainbow's end, gold solid as that mined from the Montana mountains. For river and road brought the merchandise and the men, and hauled them onward, and carried them home. At thirteen

18

cents a pound, they transported goods by the thousands of tons each season, to be loaded and unloaded along Benton's mile of shoreside levee, to be built into mountains of stores and torn down again. They brought the hordes of newcomers — hungry, tired, thirsty travelers for Benton to feed and outfit, to bed down and booze up, to profit from and push on.

Buying and selling, trading and transporting, Fort Benton liked life 1866 style. She liked her past and her present. She liked her prospects. She liked her neighbors and her newcomers. She even liked her Indians, those crazy, horse-stealing Blackfeet.

But three years later Fort Benton had turned mean. The gold mines were playing out. The Missouri was drying up. Freight charges had collapsed to two cents a pound. Furs arrived in barely a trickle. Visitors were few and broke. Money was short and tempers shorter. Desperate, the town turned to the illegal sale of whiskey to Indians. Deposing merchant and miner, the "sneaking drink giver" ruled Benton.

By 1869, the only thing keeping Fort Benton afloat was Blackfeet booze. They called it rum, and made it from a time and taste-tested recipe:

To eight quarts of muddy Missouri water add:

1 quart alcohol
1 pound rank black chewing tobacco
1 handful red peppers
1 bottle Jamaica ginger
1 quart black molasses

Mix well and boil til strength is drawn from
tobacco and peppers. Strain into kerosene tins.

The illicit trade of "rum" transformed the Ground-Of-Many-Gifts into a gutter for the Blackfeet. It debauched them. They, to whom quarreling had been unmanly and to whom loss of control had been non-human, fought among themselves and fell over in stupors. It impoverished them. The furs which should have been bartered for blankets and food all went for rum. And it inflamed them. Humiliated and ashamed, the Blackfeet became thieves. Led by the young men, angry and aroused, determined to preserve their manhood and prove their honor, bands of Blackfeet raided the white man's ranges and corrals, running off his cattle and stealing his horses.

It was in part the ancient game of warfare by night raid, but in part only. Many simply traded the stolen horses for more rum. Others ran them across the Medicine Line to Canada, there to be traded for guns and ammunition. The rest saw the raids as revenge, as just payment for the land of which they had been cheated by white whiskey traders and treaty-makers, and as retribution for the crimes committed against them.

With greedy, unprincipled whites crowding the streets and stores, and angry, aggressive Indians brawling in the bars and terrorizing the countryside, Fort Benton was ready to explode.

And on July 16, 1869, it did.

On that day, two white men rode out of town, heading west and south along the high banks of the Missouri. By mid-afternoon, far from town, as they prepared to turn back, a desperate cry for help stopped them. It came from a local cattle herder, who told them that he and his partner had been attacked by a war party of forty Indians. He had been wounded three times. His cattle had been driven off. His partner was near death.

"When the wounded men were brought into town,"

reported the Helena *Weekly Herald,* "there was great excitement."

It was an understatement.

In that long afternoon and night Bentonites executed four Piegans, two by shooting and two by hanging. "It seems the general impression here that it was the Piegans who shot the herders," wrote the *Herald.* But the impression was incorrect.

It had been River Crows and not Piegans who had attacked the herders. Worse yet, the victims of the prior day's orgy had been members of the band of Mountain-Chief, head man of all the Piegans and chief of one of the tribe's largest and most aggressive bands. One of those murdered had been his brother. Well-known and widely feared in Fort Benton, Mountain-Chief had often and openly expressed his hatred of all whites.

Once his kinship to the murdered Piegans became known, Montanans believed retaliation both imminent and certain.

"I fear before long we may have serious difficulties between Indians and whites," reported General Alfred Sully, newly-named Superintendent of Indian Affairs for Montana Territory, "and I would urge...an immediate increase of military force in Montana to prevent this."

At Fort Shaw, General Regis deTrobriand, commander of the Military District of Montana, agreed. The "quadruple murder" of the Piegans at Fort Benton, he warned, "has been the signal for new hostilities."

Convinced that every raid represented another link in the chain of revenge being forged by the aggrieved Mountain-Chief and his angry Piegan followers, Generals Alfred Sully and Regis deTrobriand waited apprehensively with the rest of Montana's citizens for what seemed the inevitable outbreak of full scale war with the Blackfeet.

I despise the whites. They have taken our land. They have killed our buffalo, which will soon pass away. They have treated my nation like dogs. I shall no longer be responsible for my young men when they seek revenge.

Mountain-Chief

Big Knives

The 19th Century Blackfeet
1830 to 1869

Many SEASONS passed between the arrival of white men in North America and their first visit to the winter camps and summer hunts of the Blackfeet. The child nation of the whites lay far from the Ground-Of-Many-Gifts, and only through Cree and Assiniboin merchant-men were beaver pelts of the Blackfeet exchanged for the metal arrowheads, thunder sticks, and bullets of Napikwan, Old-Man's-People.

But as the eighteenth century drew to a close, that was to change. Nearly two hundred years after the influence of Napikwan had first been felt on Blackfeet life in the forest, the two were to meet on the plains.

When at last the time came for meeting, it was bearded French traders who spoke for Napikwan, and from that meeting the French became Real-White-Men of the Black-feet tongue, all others imitations or imposters. Paddling northern rivers in their bark canoes, Real-White-Men brought weapons, beads, and blankets to the Blackfeet, returning to Montreal laden with the thick silky pelts of fox and beaver. English and Canadian traders followed,

Northern-White-Men to the Blackfeet, their Hudson Bay Company posts commanding strategic forks and bends of the Saskatchewan River. They traded kettles and knives, tobacco and blankets, metal arrowheads and guns.

And the potion Blackfeet called White-Man's Water — the bringer of dreams.

Warriors and kings, the Blackfeet came to Hudson Bay posts, band upon band, announced by young men and acknowledged by offerings. In ceremonial splendor they entered, emperors of the plains, and sat and smoked while their women tended lodge fires and traders poured rum. They dreamed the dreams of primitive princes and left behind them fortunes in furs.

And much more than furs. They left as well the old ways, which had been learned from the buffalo. Few remembered the oneness of life and the sufficiency of its circle when before them lay spread the wonders of Napikwan. Few remembered the long-ago days when Black-Footed-People made kettles of earth and skin, and points of arrows from stone. Napikwan made them of metal. Few recalled when women sucked and softened quills of the porcupine to decorate elkskin robes. Napikwan brought beads and blankets.

Those who saw far, the raven-visioned, warned of the danger. We are poor-minded, they said, and forgetful of our pasts. And when white scabs, the sickness Napikwan called smallpox, flamed through Blackfeet camps, they named it punishment from Sun and burned sweetgrass to cleanse their lodges and their lives. But the wonders of Napikwan were sweeter and more strong, and lingered when the sickness and the smoke had gone.

For many winters Northern-White-Men monopolized trade with the Blackfeet, shaping their lives, like the west wind, imperceptibly and irresistibly. Ever more powerful

26

the Blackfeet became, and more proud. For the gifts of the ground were inexhaustible, and purchased arsenals of weapons for the hunt and raid, displays of dazzling costumes, and lodges filled to the ears with kettles and cutlery. Many were rich, with huge herds of fine horses, sacred pipes and medicine bundles, and the bright red military jackets Napikwan gave to those he called chief. The Blackfeet felt contempt for all nations with less, and all envied their wealth and feared their power. Of all people truly the Black-Footed-People were most favored by Sun.

None felt their savage contempt more than American trappers, lured by the lodges of the Wood-Biter to violate the ground of the Blackfeet and gather its gifts. Big-Knives, the Blackfeet called them, and this became the Blackfeet name for all of the infant nation which now claimed ownership of much of their land.

Unlike Northern-White-Men, Big-Knives brought no tobacco or beads but only traps and guns, and left behind nothing in payment for their prizes. To the Blackfeet they were bandits like the Crows and Crees, pirates invading the brown, soddy sea, challenging the birthright and the bravery of its lords. And like other age-old enemies, they had to be driven off.

Let the Big-Knives learn this land belongs to the Black-Footed-People! Let them feel the earth shake to the hooves of our war ponies! Let them quake to hear Sun's power in our songs! Let them taste the bitter tongues of our lances!

The Big-Knives would see who ruled the kingdom beneath the Backbone.

It was warfare the Blackfeet knew and loved, with its raids by night and ambushes by day. Many Big-Knives sought fortune and fell, and many warriors sought glory and found graves. But many more were the coups recounted round Blackfeet lodgefires, and many more the Big-Knives made rich. There were many more victors than victims in their thirty winters of war.

But while Blackfeet braves and Big-Knife trappers warred, the merchants waited. To them would go the spoils.

Discouraged by tales of Blackfeet savagery and the remoteness of their lands, American fur trading companies stood neutral, occupied to the east. But that, too, would change. Neither the dangers nor the distance would long hold back the tide of free enterprise. Fur companies determined to penetrate the Ground-Of-Many-Gifts and establish permanent trade with the Blackfeet.

It was 1830.

*   *   *

Mountain Chief's Vision

It was in the New-Grass-Moon that I rode with a small party against a hunting band of Cutthroats. We had taken many horses and were leading them off when the camp dogs began to bark. We leaped on our ponies and flew away into the night. There was no light to guide us. Before we had reached full flight, my pony stumbled and I was thrown to the ground, my leg twisted beneath me. I called to my brothers, but the Cutthroats were close behind, and they could not stop for me. I knew I would be captured and killed. I heard the Cutthroats approaching. The hoofbeats of their ponies made the ground tremble. I was very afraid. I lay still, without moving. They did not see me, and galloped past. When I could no longer hear them, still I felt their hooves on the earth. I crawled a long distance until I came to a small gulley. There I pulled grass to cover myself and waited for the coming day.

The sun was high before the Cutthroats returned. I could see there had been a fight. Two ponies had no riders, and one warrior was wounded. They passed close enough for me to hear their voices, but again they did not see me and rode on. I wondered how my brothers had fared. All day and night I lay beneath the cover of grass, afraid to move. My leg throbbed, and I was hungry and thirsty, but I dared not move.

On the second day, I crawled from the gulley. In all directions, nothing. Only the short grass stretching to the edges of the world. I could crawl only a short way at any time. The pain in my leg was very great, and I was weak from being without food or water. I lay back, awaiting death. It was again night when I awoke. I heard an owl call, and knew its message. I prayed to Sun for my life, and vowed to undergo the ritual torture at summer encampment if I were spared. I prayed and prayed and then slept.

When I awoke, I was back in camp. I had been four days and nights on the prairie before a party of searchers found me. I told my father of my vow, and he sang and said I had done something worth doing, and would be tortured at the Sun dance.

The time until the coming together for summer encampment passed quickly. I hunted with much success, and thought little of my vow and torture. Only when the five days of building the medicine lodge began did the weight of what was to come settle on me. I spent much time alone and with my father, smoking and praying. It was on the first day following the raising of the sacred center pole that I was to be tortured. My body was painted white, with black dots under my eyes and down my arms and legs. On my forehead was a moon, around my wrists and ankles bands of sagebrush. When the painting was done, all turned away except the old man who was to cut me. He pierced my breasts with a sharp knife, pushing a short stick through each cut. Then he cut my back in two places, hanging a shield from the sticks inserted there. All was ready. Ropes hanging from the sacred center pole were tied to the sticks through my breasts. I leaned against them with all my weight and began to dance to Sun. Blood streamed over the white paint. I thought I could not bear the pain. But I did not faint, did not cry out. How long I danced I do not know, but at last the flesh tore away and I fell back on the ground. The shield was taken from my back, the ragged flaps of flesh cut from my breasts, the sagebrush bands removed. All were offered at the sacred center pole in sacrifice to Sun. Without tears, unsupported, I walked alone from the medicine lodge. I went to the sacred hill at Three Buttes, close by the summer camp, and lay waiting, alone with pain.

In the night, I found myself on top of a high hill, looking over a forest thick with trees. At the edge of the forest, I saw a great bear, whom the chosen ones call Sticky-Mouth, standing on her hind legs. Behind her, half hidden in the shadows of a cave, were her three cubs. Before her, a pack of wolves waited, without movement or sound. They were not prairie wolves, brothers to our camp dogs, brown and gray. These were like ghosts, silver and white, even their noses and paws. Only their eyes had color, and they were red as fire, flickering and burning. When the great bear charged into them, the wolves faded, floating away like puffs of smoke. And when she withdrew to shelter her cubs, they again took form on the ground before her. She raged and roared, lunged, and then returned once more to her cubs. Again and again. And always the white wolves shifted like spirits, eluding her. I knew she could not drive them off. Of what use are strength and courage against the winds? But I knew also that she would not abandon her

30

cubs, that as long as breath and blood were in her they were safe from the evil ones.

When I returned to camp, I told my father what I had seen, and he said the bear had given me power. He told me that many believe the bear is hard to kill because of his great size and keen senses, but that it was more than this. He said that of all the four-foots only Sticky-Mouth never turns and runs from his enemies. Only he fights on when danger is greatest. So must I be, he told me.

And so have I been.

*   *   *

In 1831, John Jacob Astor's American Fur Company established the first Big-Knife trading post on the Ground-Of-Many-Gifts. Located on the Missouri at the mouth of the Marias River, within the shadow of the Backbone, it was named Fort Piegan.

There Big-Knives offered the Blackfeet something Northern-White-Men could not: trade in buffalo robes. The fragile canoes of Hudson Bay Company voyageurs could not carry heavy buffalo robes in quantities sufficient to make trade profitable. The sturdy keelboats of the American Fur Company could.

And so, bound not in brotherhood but by commerce, Blackfeet and Big-Knives spent their first winter in thirty in uneasy truce.

With that winter's trade complete and spring's Thunder-Moon on the rise, the Blackfeet burned Fort Piegan to the ground. By autumn of 1832 it had been rebuilt, renamed Fort McKenzie. And the Blackfeet — awed by the stubborn will and lured by the treasures of Big-Knife traders — reappeared, hide-heavy, not to burn but for business.

*   *   *

In 1833, an eclipse of the sun darkened the Ground-Of-Many-Gifts. It was, some Blackfeet believed, a sign from Sky-Chief, a warning that the life each day reborn, the light each day bestowed upon the Black-Footed-People might one day be withheld.

But if it was a sign, it came too dimly and too late.

In the long-ago day when Napi first made man the hunter of buffalo, he warned his Black-Footed-People not to kill more than they needed, for they and the buffalo were brothers. Napi despises wasters of life, the Blackfeet had said then. But now they no longer heard Napi's word, nor heeded his warnings, so powerful was the pull of Napikwan's riches. No longer the symbol of life's oneness, of its self-sufficient circle, the buffalo-brother became victim of life's cruelty and greed, a sacrifice to its majestic madness. Naked now he lay upon the ocean of sweet short grass, abundancy intact, his fragrant meat uneaten, his splendid bones unwanted and unused, a blessing become curse, his sacred blood a stain upon the Ground-Of-Many-Gifts.

In 1837, six thousand Blackfeet died of smallpox. The survivors traded ten thousand buffalo hides at Fort Mc-Kenzie.

*   *   *

A decade later, the trade in buffalo hides had become more important to white businessman and Blackfeet hunter alike than any way of life. At Fort Benton, American Fur Company traders took in forty thousand buffalo robes from the Blackfeet each season, robes for which they could give four thousand guns, fifteen thousand blankets, forty thousand kettles, sixty thousand yards of calico, one hundred and twenty thousand knives, or one million rounds of ammunition, and still make a profit of hundreds of thousands of dollars.

As for the Blackfeet, they had long since cast their lot with the white trader and his goods. They were bound to him by a thousand chains, chains forged of metal arrow-heads, of guns and bullets, of beads and mirrors, and of rum. Had they wanted to break them, had they tried, they would have found the chains unbreakable. But they neither wanted to nor tried. They were content.

Yet even as the sacred ground slipped from beneath them, even as the old ways faded and new ways unfolded before their eyes, even then few Blackfeet could believe the dream was ending. Were not the buffalo still as thick as stars? Were not the Blackfeet many and strong? Were not they still most favored of all men? Napi had given this land to his Black-Footed-People. Sun had given them the wisdom and strength to rule it. So had it always been. So would it always be.

And still the pace accelerated. The way of life once cycled to the centuries was now measured in moments.

It was 1847.

*   *   *

In that year, Malcolm Clarke, an American Fur Company trader known to the Blackfeet as Four-Bears, took as his bride Cutting-Off-Head-Woman, from the band of Mountain-Chief.

It proved a fortuitous choice.

Mountain-Chief had grown rich and powerful. He had

many followers. They traded huge quantities of buffalo robes with their adopted brother Four-Bears, and by their example influenced other bands to trade with him also. With their backing, he grew in rank and position with the company, becoming at last virtually irreplaceable in its operations among the Blackfeet, operations by then headquartered in the new post called Fort Benton.

But many envied the success of Four-Bears. Many thought his prosperity had come at their expense. And they included most of the young Blackfeet warriors. They believed the white man and his ways doomed them never to attain positions of leadership and respect within the councils, and they were right. Traditionally, three pathways to power and prestige had been open to Blackfeet youths: warfare, the buffalo hunt, and horse-stealing. But Napikwan allowed only the profitable hunts to continue. And young Blackfeet felt frustration and anger.

Government agents preferred the conservatism of the Indian fathers to the recklessness of their sons, and it was to the elders they directed their demands that the Blackfeet walk the white man's path. It was to the elders they directed their threat that unless the young warriors abandoned the old ways, refrained from horse stealing and night raiding, the Great-White-Father would hold back the hand of friendship from his Black-Footed-Children, would bring them no food and no blankets, and would punish them for their disobedience.

And the elders were afraid and did as they were told. They knew life no longer came from Old-Man or Sky-Chief, nor from the buffalo. Life was the gift of the Great-White-Father and no other, his alone to bestow or withhold.

Among those who did not agree was Owl-Child, a

34

young warrior in the band of Mountain-Chief and cousin of Malcolm Clarke's wife, Cutting-Off-Head-Woman. His principal traits were a vicious temper and an envious nature, neither calculated to nourish affection for his cousin's prosperous white husband. Cutting-Off-Head-Woman visited often in the lodge of Owl-Child's family, accompanied by Four-Bears. And with each visit, hatred and envy of Four-Bears grew within the young warrior's heart. Owl-Child hated and envied many, but Four-Bears he hated and envied above all.

In 1864, twenty-three years old and without reputation or position, property or prospect, Owl-Child took a wife from the band of The-Heavy-Runner. In accordance with the custom of his people, he left the campfires of the band of Mountain-Chief and joined those of his new bride, among the followers of The-Heavy-Runner.

In two troubled years among The-Heavy-Runner's people, Owl-Child turned from the brashness of youth to the bitterness of the ageless. Hatred froze his heart, and burned there too, inflamed by rum. He was a man obsessed. He rode on every raid, joined every war party, less for the horses to be stolen than for the enemies to be slain. Owl-Child had become a killer, single-minded in his certainty that only with the death of his enemies might his own manhood live.

Finally the obsession overreached itself. In 1866, following a victory over a combined force of Crows and Gros Ventres, Owl-Child claimed credit for killing a Crow. Another warrior claimed the same coup and was supported by the testimony of others of the war party. Humiliated, Owl-Child murdered his rival. Following centuries of tradition, relatives of the slain warrior swore revenge upon his murderer, and Owl-Child was forced to flee his adopted band and rejoin the camp of Mountain-

Chief. Although safe there, he was in fact homeless, a renegade, an outcast among his own people.

*   *   *

The year was 1867.

Mountain-Chief had succeeded to leadership of all the Piegans, and Malcolm Clarke had retired with his Piegan wife and children to a large and prosperous ranch in the Prickly Pear Canyon, near Helena.

There, in the spring of the year, Cutting-Off-Head-Woman was visited by her Piegan relatives, among them Owl-Child.

During the visit, Owl-Child's horses were stolen, an act he considered a personal insult and vowed to avenge. That he did shortly, returning to the Clarke ranch and making off with several horses. Pursued by Four-Bears and his oldest son, Horace, Owl-Child returned to the camp of Mountain-Chief.

There the Clarkes found him.

Horace struck him with a whip and called him a dog. Four-Bears, "in words clean-cut so that all might hear," called him an old woman.

And for that Four-Bears would die.

None among the Blackfeet doubted that fact, not even those who hated and distrusted Owl-Child, as much as they wished to avoid conflict with the whites. Owl-Child's manhood had been challenged. He would be avenged. Four-Bears would die.

*   *   *

With the murders of the four Piegans in Fort Benton on July 16, 1869, war councils were called throughout the

36

camps of the Blackfeet. Some urged forbearance. It was the act of a few men, crazed by rum, they told their brothers. To punish them we risk all, our lodges and our lives. But many more voices spoke for revenge. And among them the loudest was Mountain-Chief's.

Are Blackfeet men, he asked, or cringing dogs, to be kicked by the whites and chased away? Who dares challenge the Blackfeet, he shouted, must die! Let there be war!

And there might have been war, but for an intervention from the spirit world. On August 7, 1869, Sun again hid his face from his people of the plains.

For those who remembered the day thirty-five years before, when an eclipse of the sun had darkened the Ground-Of-Many-Gifts, and who would never forget the scourge of white scabs which had followed, the sign was unmistakable. There must be no war with the whites.

But Owl-Child knew that for him there could be no peace.

Malcolm Clarke lived still and must die. Not in revenge for the murder of four Piegans at Fort Benton. Not as a random slaying in an impersonal pattern of depredations. Not as an act of war. Four-Bears would die in satisfaction of a debt. Owl-Child chose the confusion, the anger and the fear of August 18, 1869, to cloak the deed.

On that night, accompanied by several other young warriors, among them a son of Mountain-Chief, Owl-Child visited once more the ranch in Prickly Pear Canyon. There he shot and killed Four-Bears. Mountain-Chief's son seriously wounded Horace.

Owl-Child's revenge was complete. Learning of the incident, Mountain-Chief expressed neither surprise nor interest. "The trouble," he said, "was between Owl-Child and Four-Bears. It does not concern us."

I fear we will have to consider the Blackfeet in a state of war.

General Alfred Sully
August 18, 1869

The Blackfeet...remain still perfectly quiet, protesting...that they want no war, but peace.

General Regis deTrobriand
September 9, 1869

Whiskey is at the bottom of all the trouble...

War or Peace?
August 18 to December 27, 1869

WHEN NEWS OF Four-Bears' murder first reached Generals Alfred Sully and Regis deTrobriand, they agreed on its import.

"I fear we will have to consider the Blackfeet in a state of war," Sully cabled Indian Commissioner Ely Parker. "Indians on the warpath," deTrobriand echoed. "Applications for protection in men and arms coming upon me from all sides."

Those applications held a real problem for deTrobriand.

"The Major General commanding knows how I am situated to answer those appeals," he pointed out. "Until recruits have arrived I must remain passive — whatever may happen — having not even a sufficient number of men to protect my own posts."

The men of Montana, however, persisted.

41

"Citizens from different sections...have visited me asking permission to take the law with regard to Indians into their own hands," Sully reported, "on the plea that there are no military forces in the country to protect them."

Montana Governor James Ashley heard the same pleas. "A number of citizens have called and requested me to issue a proclamation calling for a volunteer force to go after the Indians," he wrote deTrobriand on August 21, adding: "This I have declined doing until I can be shown that you have no force at your command sufficient to protect peaceably disposed citizens."

Regis deTrobriand was justifiably concerned. Unless he convinced his superiors of the necessity for immediate reinforcements in substantial numbers, his control of military operations in Montana could be lost.

"In case of emergency the present condition of this command is ridiculously disproportioned with the calls made, or to be made, upon it," he complained on August 24. Without more troops, he warned, "the government will have, I fear, to send some force from other quarters or to pay for a regiment of mounted volunteers, which will be a great deal of trouble and expense."

But time was running out. Rumor that the Piegans had evacuated their women and children to camps north of the Medicine Line in Canada "is significant," reported the *Helena Weekly Herald* on August 26, "and means war. That we are on the verge of a general Indian outbreak no sensible man who understands the situation can deny."

"The pleasant and innocent amusement of butchering and scalping the pale-faces," it added, "is believed by some likely soon to begin in good earnest."

Furthermore, the *Herald* viewed with pessimism the Army's ability to prevent the anticipated slaughter, pointing out that "the military force...is small, and altogether inadequte to active operations, should that course against the Indians be required."

Community pressure focused on Governor Ashley, who could only at growing cost maintain his opposition to the enlistment of volunteers.

"I am loudly denounced and condemned by many because I have not called out the militia or authorized irresponsible bodies of men to take the public arms and go after and punish the Indians," he cabled Secretary of the Interior Jacob Cox.

Montana's impatient frontiersmen were not to be put off. They wanted action, and wanted it now. But to whom could they turn? Who would heed their appeals? On August 26, the *Herald* offered a suggestion.

"We are well satisfied that with a force of four or five regiments armed and equipped in accordance with General Sully's mode of Indian warfare, he would soon put an end to these outrages," the paper editorialized, "and give the red devils a whipping that would last for all time to come."

In the minds of Montanans, not Regis deTrobriand but Alfred Sully should be commanding general of Montana. Not Regis deTrobriand but Alfred Sully should have responsibility for defending the whites and punishing the Indians of the Ground-Of-Many-Gifts.

Alfred Sully had nothing against the idea.

Alfred Sully's Vision

Five years earlier, on July 28, 1864, Alfred Sully stood at the head of the most powerful army ever assembled to fight Indians on the American plains. Arrayed by regiment, its four thousand eight hundred volunteer cavalrymen and their mounts prepared to take the field against a formidable foe. Behind them lay a month-long march, which had brought the huge force and its equally-expansive escort (three hundred supply wagons, a vast herd of cattle, and fifteen supporting steamboats back along the Missouri and Yellowstone rivers, plus a wagon train of two hundred and fifty west-bound emigrants) from Fort Ridgeley in Minnesota to this battleground on the border of Dakota and Montana territories at the base of Kildeer Mountain. Before them stood what seemed the whole of the Sioux nation — six thousand warriors, freshly mounted and fully armed. For the Indian wars, it was an encounter of staggering proportions, epic in appeal, rivaling in scope many of the contemporary engagements between North and South.

From it Alfred Sully won his reputation as the greatest Indian fighter of the 1860s.

In reality, Sully's reputation would rest less on the daring of his combat leadership, or the fighting prowess of his troops, than on the impact of a battery of twelve field artillery pieces, which for the first time accompanied troops into action against the Indians. These were not the ineffective cannons which more decorated than protected most frontier forts, but massive horse-drawn howitzers with long range and reasonable accuracy. Sully had long advocated their use against the Indians. The sound alone of massed artillery would spread terror among a primitive people, he argued, to say nothing of the frighteningly destructive force of the weapon itself.

And he was right.

Confident in the superiority of their numbers, marksmanship, and mounts, the Sioux attacked. Equally sure of his artillery, Sully waited until the warriors were well

44

within range before opening fire. One hundred and fifty Indians died in the first salvo. With the second, the remainder broke and ran. Sully's men suffered scarcely a casualty, and without further opposition entered the Sioux summer camp, destroying fifteen hundred lodges and the fruits of a summer's hunt.

For the Sioux, the Battle of Kildeer Mountain was a disastrous defeat. For Alfred Sully, it was not just the climax of a long and arduous campaign, but the pinnacle of a career.

Yet within a week the positions of victor and vanquished seemed certain to be reversed, and quickly.

By early August, the mammoth army of the plains was lost in the badlands of the Dakotas, its ranks depleted by exhaustion and burning heat, its cattle dying for lack of food and water, its vehicles slowed by sands and disabled by boulders.

"Hell with the fires put out," Sully described the barren badlands, as his army, its recent triumph all but forgotten, trudged up uncharted chasms and down blind arroyos, and cursed the parties of Sioux warriors who pursued and taunted them in their agony. Only the threat of Sully's big guns prevented an all-out assault, keeping the Sioux dancing just out of range, darting in only to be gone again before the unwieldy artillery could be wheeled into place, loaded, aimed, and fired. Kildeer Mountain seemed many months and miles behind the mightiest army the plains had ever seen.

At last, on August 7, Sully acted to break the impasse that threatened to drain the last ounce of will from his flagging troops, personally leading them through three days of fierce fighting to struggle out of the seemingly endless bottoms of the badlands. By August 9 they had gained their objective, reaching high ground, driving before them the Sioux warriors. It had been a close contest, with the outcome neither so dramatic nor so decisive as that at Kildeer Mountain. Yet it had been a victory well-earned after a battle hard-fought, and Alfred Sully's stature suffered not in the least.

When Sully and his army reached the Yellowstone River and a rendezvous with their steamboats, news of their triumph at the Battle of the Badlands had preceded them. The crews cheered their arrival.

In 1864, Alfred Sully, conqueror of the Sioux, was a national hero.

But with peace at Appomattox, his glory dimmed.

First, William Tecumseh Sherman, then Philip Henry Sheridan, and finally George Custer came to the frontier, and in April 1866 an already overshadowed Alfred Sully left it. Not until March of 1868 did he return to plains duty at Fort Harker, Kansas, reporting to Sheridan.

It was the beginning of the end of a long and distinguished military career.

"Cautious and slow-moving," Sheridan described Sully, making clear his aversion to such traits in the military character. Sheridan preferred Custer's reckless, aggressive style, and disliked working with the older, slower, though still-popular Indian fighter.

Their problems began quickly. In July 1868, the bands of Kiowa and Comanche camped near Fort Larned were denied a promised issue of arms and ammunition by their agent. As a consequence they staged round-the-clock war dances and otherwise threatened the undermanned outpost.

"Sully thought that the delivery of the arms would solve all the difficulties," Sheridan wrote, "so on his advice the agent turned them over along with the annuities."

Immediately the Indians took to the war path with their

46

newly-issued weapons, terrorizing the surrounding settlements and enraging Sheridan.

"This issue of arms and ammunitions was a fatal mistake," he said. "Indian diplomacy had overreached Sully's experience."

It was a crushing criticism of the frontier's foremost Indian fighter, and Sully was determined to counter it with vigorous retaliation against the offending Kiowa and Comanche.

But it was not to be. Pursuing the war parties to the Cimarron River, he was there overwhelmed and driven back to Fort Dodge.

Sully "had marched up the hill and then, like the forces of the king of France, had marched down again," commented Custer.

"I think," wrote William Tecumseh Sherman, "Sully made a botch of it."

Though humiliated, one last opportunity remained to salvage Sully's sinking reputation. Sheridan determined to mount the first winter campaign in the history of the plains against the offending Indians, and he placed Sully in command, superior even to Custer, with initial orders to march his troops to Fort Dodge.

While on that march, Custer discovered a fresh Indian trail and requested Sully's permission to follow. Sully denied the request, an act which Custer promptly reported to Sheridan.

To Sheridan, this was the last straw. Angered, he relieved Sully of the combat command, returning him to his desk at Fort Harker. Custer took over the battle column.

Shortly thereafter Sully was relieved of military command, assigned to the Department of the Interior for civilian duty, and in May of 1869 he became Montana's Superintendent of Indian Affairs.

When the events of autumn in Montana held promise of restoring the luster of his name and the ascendency of his military career, the temptation to promote those events was strong indeed.

Alfred Sully couldn't resist.

*   *   *

Alfred Sully's ambitions had found new hope, his spirits new confidence. Buoyed by a widening circle of supporters and sustained by their apparent certainty of purpose and assurances of success, the reinvigorated Indian fighter continued to insist that the Blackfeet were indeed at war, to press the necessity of prompt military response to their aggressions, and to maintain both positions in the face of opinion to the contrary from more objective observers of the Blackfeet Nation.

"There is so far only a small band of the Piegans that are or that have been interested in the depredations lately committed," reported his agent to the Blackfeet on August 31, "and their moving north with their families has been caused by fear of being accused of having something to do with these depredations, and the false reports of irresponsible, mischief-making whites."

Trader Alexander Culbertson, a veteran of four decades of dealings with the Piegans, supported the agent's view.

"My knowledge of their character for a great many years will not permit me to think that there exists a general hostile feeling among them," he wrote Sully on September 2. "On the contrary, these depredations have been committed by a portion of the young rabble, over whom the chiefs have no control."

Unwilling to give circulation to points of view which might delay or even prevent the general campaign which

48

had by now become his fervent hope, Sully ignored the reports. Cautiously, avoiding confrontation with deTrobriand or open advocacy of the volunteer force, he waited.

Regis deTrobriand, meanwhile, fumed. Only one officer could command military affairs in Montana, and while he had the title, it appeared that Sully might soon have the troops. That deTrobriand had not the regular forces at his disposal to respond to the Blackfeet threat was a matter of public record. That he opposed the enlisting of a volunteer force was equally well known. And to openly accuse Sully of attempting to usurp his military authority would only bring convincing denial. Frustrated, he continued to petition his superiors for additional troops, troops enough to convince the impatient Montanans that he could himself challenge and punish the Blackfeet.

Unfortunately for deTrobriand, his pleas for reinforcement had fallen on deaf ears all along the chain of command, culminating in Sheridan's report of September 8 to General of the Army William Tecumseh Sherman that there was nothing to be concerned about.

"General deTrobriand is somewhat excited on the subject," Sheridan told Sherman, "and I have but little doubt the Governor would like to call out a regiment of volunteers, but he will receive no encouragement from me.

"I think the thing will worry through the winter."

Thwarted in his efforts to secure additional troops, the beleaguered deTrobriand at last decided to concentrate his energies on the one factor which might be open to his influence: the belief by Montanans that they teetered on the brink of disaster at the hands of the Blackfeet. Departing on an inspection tour in late August, determined to change that belief, he returned to Fort Shaw two weeks later with a detailed report to the effect that the Blackfeet, far from wishing war, had rarely been more peaceful.

"The Blackfeet...the Bloods, and even part of the Piegans, remain still perfectly quiet," he reported on September 7, "protesting that they have nothing to do with the attacks... that they want no war, but peace, and that they are ready to come and stay on whatever reservation may be assigned to them."

As for the continuing predictions of war, said deTrobriand, "I strongly suspect that there was some interested scheme on the part of some parties to magnify the danger, exaggerate the reports, and through the general excitement to bring the Governor to issue a proclamation to raise a regiment of mounted volunteers.

"This, if successful," he added, "would have procured some fat jobs to somebody or other at the expense of the government."

(Montana offered precedent for deTrobriand's suspicions. In 1866, Governor Thomas Meagher had recruited a volunteer militia to fight the Blackfeet, and "succeeded only," commented one historian, "in disturbing those who might normally become apprehensive over the military enthusiasm of a citizen army. For this service the government was billed over a million dollars." "The biggest humbug of the age," agreed Augustus Chapman, agent to the Flathead Indians, "got up to advance his political interest, and to enable a lot of bummers who surround and hang on to him to make a big raid on the United States Treasury.")

But others did not share deTrobriand's opposition to volunteer forces, or his sanguine view of the Indian situation in Montana.

"It will be no fault of the Government and certain belligerent parties if we are spared the horrors of a general war," wrote the *Herald* on September 23.

"The commanders of military posts in this Territory do

not seem to realize the situation," the paper went on, commenting that while some had "exerted themselves to the utmost to have troops sent here...their efforts have been neutralized...by the actions of commanding officers who, we are informed, represent to headquarters that these difficulties are magnified by designing men for purposes of speculation."

These statements brought the *Herald* to the point of its editorial:

"We hope soon to see a change for the better. Upon hearing of the appointment of General Sully to this Superintendency, we ventured to hope that he would have command of the troops in this district, and that there would be a sufficient force at his disposal to produce some beneficial results: but he is powerless, except to make and carry out treaties.

"We need an officer like the General in this district, and we regard it as a misfortune that he cannot be placed in command of the troops as well as the Indians. Then he could either feed or

Swept along by such public approval, Alfred Sully carried out his part in support of the position that Indian affairs in Montana had reached the crisis stage. From each encounter he wrung the last drop of evidence or opinion favorable to the cause of action.

"The Indians have now been at this work for over two months," he reported on September 27, "and as no one...made any attempt whatever to check them, they are daily becoming more bold in their operations."

Furthermore, said Sully, if the government opposed a volunteer force on the basis of unnecessary expense, it should be made aware that other costs had already been incurred.

"There are already over four hundred horses and mules

known to have been stolen lately," he pointed out. "That number, at $150 each, will make an expensive claim against the government."

If the government refused to be concerned over the loss of life, perhaps legal claims for $60,000 might move it.

*　　*　　*

On the evening of September 29, 1869, the aroused citizens of Helena met publicly, determined to bring matters to a head.

The most militant supported a proposal by the chief of police "to arm and equip his men at his own expense, provided they receive a reward for every scalp taken, and be allowed to own all the property taken from the Indians."

Cooler heads prevailed temporarily, however, and it was decided to table the police chief's plan pending a response from Regis deTrobriand to a last appeal for military·protection.

"The committee have concluded, as the first step in this matter, to ask you to put into the field two hundred cavalry," the petition read, "and drive to their reservations...the Indians now scattered through the Territory; and that, having done this, you will station parties of troops for the time being at the principal passes through which they are wont to make their incursions."

"We do this," the appeal concluded, "not in a spirit of dictation or fault-finding, but believing that you are anxious to cooperate with us in staying the ruthless band threatening our homes and firesides."

The earnestness of the citizens of Helena, however, paled before the dedication of Regis deTrobriand. Life and livestock were seen by the settlers to be in peril. Rank and reputation comprised deTrobriand's stake. With so much more in the balance, he replied to his petitioners on October 6.

"Let us see the facts as they are, and without exaggeration," he wrote.

"The first fact, which I think must be admitted by all, is that there is no Indian war in the Territory."

As for the second fact, deTrobriand went on, it could best be explained by "a French proverb, which says that the prettiest girl can give but what she has! So with any military commander. He cannot furnish more troops than he has under his command."

The conclusion was inescapable:

"I must therefore candidly inform your honorable committee that the plan of operations suggested in their communication is utterly impracticable."

If the citizens of Helena had any idea that the Frenchman with the unpronounceable name would accede to their demands or stand aside for their famous old Indian fighter, they underestimated their adversary.

*　　*　　*

Regis deTrobriand's Vision

One fateful afternoon in 1861, Philippe Régis Dénis de Keredern deTrobriand, son of Baron Joseph Vincent Pierre Marie Dénis de Keredern deTrobriand and Jeanne Rose Hachin de Courbeville, looked out the window of his New York apartment to see a regiment of Massachusetts volunteers marching off to join the Union Army, and thought "of those familiar sights of my childhood, when the French battalions defiled before the starry epaulets of my father, and I wondered vaguely if the destiny that had deprived me of the heritage of his sword had not in reserve for me in America some compensation, in the ranks of these volunteers marching to fight for a cause which had immortalized Lafayette."

It, of course, had.

Lawyer and poet, painter, novelist, journalist, musician and bon vivant, world traveler, and above all, aristocrat, Regis deTrobriand became, on August 28, 1861, a citizen of the United States and commanding officer of the 55th New York Volunteers — the Lafayette Escadrille.

True to four centuries of family tradition, he had by war's end distinguished himself with the Army of the Potomac at the campaigns of Fredericksburg, Chancellorsville, Gettysburg, and Appomattox; had risen to the position of Grant's chief of artillery and the rank of major general with the volunteers (joining Lafayette as the only Frenchmen ever to hold so high a rank in the U.S. Army); and in 1866 was in Paris writing a book titled *Four Years of Campaigns In The Army of The Potomac.* There he received notice of his appointment to the Regular Army and his orders to assume command of the 31st New York Regiment on duty in Dakota Territory. On June 11, 1867, his book completed and in the hands of publishers, Regis deTrobriand again took leave of his native land, this time for Indian country.

"From the brilliant peaks of civilized life," he wrote, "I was to plunge straight into the dark pit of savage existence"

Whatever truth it may have contained, it was an unfortunate point of view to bring to the Dakota of 1867, to its plains and its peoples.

Its plains, in fact, he liked. "They give," he wrote, "...an impression of immensity, of open space, and of an individual left to his own resources in the midst of nature where nothing belongs to anyone and everything belongs to everyone." He felt, he said, a "feeling of freedom under the sun that almost always exults one."

But the people of the Dakota plains were another matter. White or red, civilian or soldier, deTrobriand despised them all.

Of the Indian he wrote:

"Neither heaven nor earth cause a poetic fiber to vibrate in him, for he has none, and the lack of all sentiments of this kind in him is so marked that he does not even sing about the great deeds of the hunt or of war, and is ignorant of the art of inflaming the ardor or ambition of young warriors and of preserving the memory of his heroes. Impossible to be more prosaic. Oh, Chateaubriand, where is your noble savage!"

And of whites:

"If theft, deceit, murder, and war have come...the fault is definitely that of the whites alone. The trading posts...multiplied rapidly...the great profits from the trade bred rivalries among the traders; these rivalries resulted in stratagems of all sorts and perfidies by which each made great efforts to attract the Indians and to turn them away from competitors. So to harm one another, the whites began to stir up the Indians and encouraged them to steal. The redskins learned from them bad faith, then theft, then the murder of the traders or their employees. Whiskey was introduced among them to encourage them in evil and to despoil them more easily. So Pandora's box was opened on the plains, and the vice, injustice, and bad treatment sown by the whites produced this bloody harvest, which for ten years had cost so much in blood and money."

Civilian Indian Agents drew his wrath:

"And here are the Indians, plundered, robbed, and mercilessly oppressed by the agents of the government.

Let us hope that all this trash from the Indian Bureau will soon be cleaned out."

And if venality and corruption marked the actions of civilians, deTrobriand was even more disgusted by the drunkenness and brutality of his fellow officers. At Fort Totten, he wrote, three of five officers were drunkards, adding:

"When the commandant is drunk, which is almost every day, he gives himself over to his ridiculous or brutal eccentricities, which, of course, earn him the hatred and scorn of his men. One can imagine the state of discipline and the condition of the service when authority is in such hands."

"The drunkards will be swept with one stroke from my corps of officers," he vowed, "...for I will not tolerate one of them in my regiment as long as I command it."

But the drunkards would not be swept away, nor would any others of the offending peoples of the frontier command. For the duration of his tours on the plains, Regis deTrobriand would be confronted over and over again with unfeeling savages and unprincipled whites, corrupt civilians and corrupted soldiers.

He was not a man well suited by temperment or breeding for such encounters.

Entering the sixth decade of his life, he had experienced nothing to suggest that his feelings of superiority were other than appropriate and justified. By birth and background, by intellect and education, by rank and position, Regis deTrobriand simply assumed his superiority and its universal acknowledgment, assumed that respect would always be his without question.

And he was always surprised when it was not.

"Is it not strange," he wrote to his son-in-law, "that being so fond of peace, as I am, I find so often in my way some confounded fellow who will bring me out for a fight in some way or other."

Among those "confounded fellows" were the Imperial Procurer of France; General Winfield Scott Hancock; the Governor of Utah (a "whipped dog," deTrobriand called him); and the Sioux Indian agent (whom deTrobriand accused of "impudence raised to the third power").

And so it was once again with surprise, though scarcely inexperience, that Regis deTrobriand encountered the challenges of October 1869 from the renegade Blackfeet and the presuming Alfred Sully.

The Indians presented the lesser threat. Long ago he had articulated the military tactic to be employed against them.

"Range far out during the winter to surprise the permanent villages where the tribes keep their women and children," he advocated. "The confessed aim is to exterminate everyone, for this is the only advantage of making the expedition; if extermination were not achieved, just another burden would be added — prisoners."

The time was not far off when he would put the tactic to the test.

As for Sully, he would pay for his presumption. It was a price to be paid by any who questioned the four-hundred-year-old deTrobriand motto:

Trop Brillant Pour Etre Terni — "Too Bright To Tarnish."

*   *   *

On the ninth of October, 1869, the Honorable G.G. Symes, judge of the Third Judicial District of the Territory of Montana, speaking for a recently convened United States Grand Jury, issued a general indictment of the

Blackfeet Indians and specific warrants for the arrest of five Piegan warriors in the murder of Malcolm Clarke and the near-fatal assault on his son Horace.

"We believe from our own knowledge and the evidence adduced," the indictment read, "that within six months fully 1,000 horses have been stolen and a number of valuable citizens sacrificed.

"The Blackfeet nation have moved their women and children north of Montana into British Possessions, for their safety, and in that country have procured supplies and ammunition and improved arms. This is a declaration of war on the whites of Montana by these Indians."

"Ours is a contest between civilization and barbarism," the indictment concluded, "and we must risk our lives and sacrifice our hard-earned property to defend them unless the general government gives us the means of defense."

Attached to the indictment were warrants for the arrest of Owl-Child, Eagle's-Rib, Black-Bear, Bear-Chief, and Black-Weasel.

Montanans approved wholeheartedly of the Grand Jury's actions, for, as the *Helena Weekly Herald* pointed out, "the Indian is amenable to courts for any grave offense, the same as the white man, and this is one of the ways by which, in many instances, our people can bring to justice and the gallows Indian assassins and robbers whose names are known and who can be identified by witnesses."

It was not judges and juries, however, but generals who would bring justice to the Blackfeet, and many miles east of Montana that process had begun in earnest.

In Washington, Indian Commissioner Ely Parker assembled the alarming correspondence from his Montana Indian Superintendent and forwarded it to Secretary of the Interior Jacob Cox with the following notation: "This bureau is powerless to control and prevent these depredations, and I respectfully suggest the communications be referred to the Secretary of War, with the request that the military take prompt measures to check them."

Cox took the advice and on October 12 forwarded the reports to General of the Army Sherman, indicating that they clearly set forth "the necessity of prompt action by the military to check the depredations," and requesting that "further reinforcements of the military force in that Territory be made."

Sherman in turn sent the reports the same day to his Missouri Division Commander Philip Sheridan, ordering him to take "such action as the case calls for."

Although on record earlier that "the thing will worry through the winter," Sheridan acknowledged the order without question, and within ten days sent his recommendation to Sherman.

"I think it would be the best plan to let me find out exactly where these Indians are going to spend the winter," he cabled on October 21, "and about the time of a good heavy snow I will send out a party and try to strike them.

"We might be able to give them a good hard blow, which will make peace a desirable object.

"To simply keep troops on the defensive will not stop the murders," Sheridan pointed out. "We must occasionally strike where it hurts."

On November 4, 1869, Sherman authorized Sheridan to deliver his "good hard blow" against the Blackfeet. "I have the honor to inform you," he cabled, "that your proposed action for the punishment of these marauders has been approved."

There would be now no turning back.

Far from the frontier, the decision had been made. Regis

deTrobriand was no longer in danger of being unhorsed, and Alfred Sully had no longer any hope of assuming the reins. If anyone was going to punish the Blackfeet, it would be the United States Army.

And if any man in the United States Army knew how to punish Indians, that man was Philip Sheridan.

*   *   *

Philip Sheridan's Vision

As Chief of Cavalry for the Army of the Potomac, Philip Henry Sheridan epitomized the dash and daring of the horseman-warrior. Astride his jet-black stallion, Rienzi, he stampeded Southern armies up and down the Shenandoah Valley — first Jeb Stuart, crown jewel of the Confederate Cavalry; then Jubal Early, the bold, resourceful raider; and finally Robert E. Lee himself, stalwart rock of the rebellion.

"Sheridan was more than magnetic," wrote a war correspondent. "He was electric."

With the surrender of the South and the completion of an interim civil assignment, Sheridan was ordered in August 1867 to carry the force of his charge onto the Great Plains.

His first assignment required him to round up twenty thousand Cheyenne, Arapaho, Comanche, Kiowa, and Kiowa-Apache Indians scattered over one hundred fifty thousand square miles of southern and central plains — Indians crowded by settlers, cheated by traders, manipulated by treaties, and harrassed by troops — and confine them to two new reservations. To get the job done he had twenty-six hundred troops, some of them mutinous, many of them alcoholic, most of them untrained, all of them lonely and underpaid.

It was a difficult task, and Sheridan took a six-month leave before settling down to it.

By the spring of 1868, he was ready. At the peak of his not inconsiderable powers, and convinced that "Indians must be terribly whipped before they can appreciate kindness," he determined a course that would revolutionize plains warfare.

"I made up my mind to confine operations during the grazing and hunting season to protecting the people of the new settlements and on the overland routes," he wrote, "and then, when winter came, to fall upon the savages relentlessly, for in that season their ponies would be thin and weak from lack of food, and in the cold and snow, without strong ponies to transport their villages and plunder, their movements would be so much impeded that the troops could overtake them."

It had never been done. His superiors doubted it could be. Veteran frontiersmen *knew* it couldn't. Anyone familiar with the cruel cold and blinding blizzards of plains winters knew that the few soldiers who weren't lost, frozen, or starved along the way would be too weak to fight if they ever encountered an Indian. But what was the impossible to the man whose troops had stormed Missionary Ridge — "one of the greatest miracles of military history"?

"Destroy their villages and ponies," Sheridan ordered General George Custer (who had earlier replaced Alfred Sully as Force Commander). "Kill or hang all warriors and bring back all women and children."

On November 27, 1868, at the Battle of Washita River, Custer carried out the order. And it worked. Black Kettle and more than one hundred of his Cheyenne warriors were killed, fifty of his women and children captured. In a frenzy of auditing, Custer reported the destruction:

875 horses	4000 arrows
241 saddles	75 spears
573 buffalo robes	90 bullet molds
390 buffalo skins	35 bows and quivers
160 untanned robes	12 shields
210 axes	300 pounds of bullets
140 hatchets	775 lariats
35 revolvers	940 saddlebags
47 rifles	93 coats
535 pounds of powder	700 pounds of tobacco

1050 pounds of lead

"The blow struck was a most effective one," Sheridan wrote, "and, fortunately, fell on one of the most villainous of the hostile bands that, without any provocation whatever, perpetrated the massacres...committing atrocities too repulsive for recital, and whose hands were still red from their bloody work."

The plan had succeeded just as he had known it would, and on January 2, 1869, he delivered his ultimatum to the surviving chiefs: "You may say to the Cheyennes and Arapahoes that I will stick to what I am going to say, and they can believe every word of it. I do not care one cent, as far as I am concerned myself, whether they come in or stay out. If they stay out, I will make war on them winter and summer as long as I live, or until they are wiped out."

In March 1869, this became official policy for all of the plains. With Grant in the White House and Sherman the new General of the Army, Sheridan became commander of the Division of the Missouri, replacing Sherman.

By autumn, when informed of the Blackfeet rebellion, he had no doubt what would best serve the case.

*   *   *

On November 6, Alfred Sully received news of Sheridan's plan for punishing the Blackfeet, and it moderated his earlier estimates of the Indian threat.

"It appears to be the impression among those acquainted with these Indians that they do not intend a general war," he reported on November 16.

"Whiskey is at the bottom of all the trouble," he wrote. "If troops patrol the country...and if commanding officers of posts will use all their energy to stop the whiskey traders, I believe we will have little difficulty."

All Piegan bands together totalled no more than 800 fighting men, Sully calculated, and Mountain-Chief's band — "said to be the worst" — numbered only 60 lodges, or no more than 180 warriors.

"At any rate, it is not thought here that there will be any serious trouble til next spring."

But it was too late.

On the same day Sheridan was notified that his plan had been approved, he alerted General Winfield Scott Hancock, Regis deTrobriand's immediate superior, that a winter campaign against the Blackfeet would be mounted.

The news came as a surprise to Hancock.

His knowledge of Indian affairs in Montana came from deTrobriand, who had assured him always that matters were well under control, that calls to arms came only from self-serving politicians and cries for aid only from irrationally fearful settlers.

And now here was Sheridan ordering him to prepare for a mid-winter expedition.

Hancock's suspicions had been roused earlier by the U.S. Grand Jury indictment and warrants which had crossed his desk, and he had written deTrobriand, demanding to know how the citizens of Helena could be so alarmed while deTrobriand remained so calm. Hancock had not yet received a reply, but now Sheridan's communication confirmed that the Blackfeet situation was far more troubled than he had been led to believe. Confused and concerned, he ordered deTrobriand on November 10 to "make all possible endeavors to ascertain where the offending Blackfeet are wintering."

It was only as an apparent afterthought that he commented, "If we can get at the Indians during the winter, by a quick, active march, we might surprise their camps."

Unaware that a campaign against the Blackfeet had in fact been ordered, deTrobriand in the meantime received Hancock's earlier communiqué, and set out once more to demonstrate that Montanans had no cause for alarm. "All has been perfectly quiet everywhere," he reported. "No serious difficulties are to be apprehended for the winter."

As for the citizens of Helena, he explained, he had asked them to "promptly advise me of any new disturbances that might come to their knowledge" — something they had been unable to do, "since none occurred."

By November 22, deTrobriand still had no word of the campaign and still believed the interests of his career best served by minimizing the threat from the Blackfeet. "So many false and exaggerated reports are spread... respecting the Indians in Montana," he wrote to Hancock, "that I deem it my duty to report any fact, even of minor importance, which may contribute to an appreciation of the true condition of things." In that spirit, he announced that the murder of one James Quail, earlier attributed by Alfred Sully to the Blackfeet, "...was, according to all probabilities and circumstantial evidence, committed by white men, and that the Indians had nothing whatever to do with it."

What's more, he added, "any report of Indian disturbances in this district since that date up to the present time is absolutely false, and without foundation whatever."

*   *   *

By the time he responded to Hancock's cable of November 10, however, Regis deTrobriand, too, had reason to be confused. Several hundred new recruits had at last arrived at his Fort Shaw headquarters, and he didn't know who had sent them or why. Still without knowledge of the scheduled winter mission, he could only conjecture that Hancock intended them for the "quick, active march" hinted at in the cable. And still of the opinion that he had most to gain from minimizing the dangers, he made short work of that idea.

"I do not see," he told Hancock on November 26, "an opportunity for striking a successful blow.

"The only Indians within reach are decidedly friendly, and nothing could be worse, I think, than to chastise them for offenses of which they are not guilty."

Expanding on the theme, deTrobriand reported the locations of the winter camps of the Blackfeet.

"The Piegans are divided. The main body is now in the British Territory, hunting and trading. It is thought that they will come back early in the spring to join the other band, if nothing frightens them away.

"The other band is friendly, under the lead of The-Heavy-Runner, their chief. It is much the smaller of the two.

"Mountain-Chief, whose son shot the young Horace Clarke, is with a small band roaming along Milk River, on or beyond the frontier line. Black-Weasel is with him.

"Owl-Child is the worst ruffian among the Indians. The last heard of him he was with a small band of Bloods on the Marias River. He is the one I wish most to have, dead or alive, as his punishment would be the most telling example."

Eagle's-Rib and "other Piegans implicated in the murders and depredations of last summer keep away in different directions," deTrobriand reported, while the Bloods and Northern Blackfeet had settled down north of the border and were likely to remain there for the winter.

"Let everything remain quiet and in the spring they will come back," he predicted. "Then I think will be the best chance to give them a lesson of good effect."

It was not until December 5 that deTrobriand received official notification from Hancock of the orders committing him and his troops to the winter campaign against the Blackfeet.

"About the time of a good heavy snow," the orders read, "send out a command and endeavor to strike them a blow." January 15 was suggested as a likely day and Major Eugene M. Baker recommended as the appropriate commander.

"General Sheridan says he is competent," Hancock wrote.

But if deTrobriand's questions regarding the purpose of his reinforcements had been answered and his choices reduced to "having everything in readiness to strike at the appointed time," he had nonetheless too often been on record as opposed to action against the Blackfeet to now make more than an uneasy commitment to the campaign.

"The only hostile band which may be within reach at the time appointed (unless some improbable change occurs before)," he told Hancock, "is the one of Mountain-Chief. It is against them that I propose to direct the expedition. They have no village, but a small moving camp, and I apprehend that it will not be so easy to catch them as it would have been a little later on the Marias River where they intend to come if all be quiet.

"If they do it as early as the beginning of January," deTrobriand continued, "it will be all right. If not, it may turn out that the expedition has been premature."

Finally, he suggested that the campaign be referred to in future communications as the "winter drill" to prevent its becoming public knowledge.

"I shall," he said, "understand what that means."

*   *   *

While Regis deTrobriand prepared his plan for war against the Blackfeet, Alfred Sully was preparing a new plan of his own for peace.

"Two hundred lodges expected soon on the Marias. Say they want peace," he reported to Indian Commissioner Parker on December 6. "A demand for the murderers and stolen property, backed with a military force, would be acceded to."

Parker liked the idea and forwarded it promptly to Sherman.

"I think the demand suggested by General Sully should be made," he told the General of the Army, "but to make it effective, the cooperation of the military may be required. I would therefore...request that you cause instructions to be given for the military at Forts Shaw and Benton to hold themselves in readiness to assist General Sully, if found necessary."

Sherman approved and on December 13 ordered deTrobriand to "furnish Gen. Sully with what military assistance he may require to support any demand he may make," and to "place troops at such points as he may indicate."

Regis deTrobriand was horrified, his worst fears realized

at the very moment he had believed them finally over-come. Having successfully prevented Sully from recruiting a pack of irregulars, he was now ordered to relinquish control of his own troops to the old Indian fighter.

For his part, Alfred Sully could afford to be charitable, and in a private communication he attempted to persuade deTrobriand to his point of view.

"As you said, I did send for the chiefs to talk with," he wrote, but "do not propose to pitch into them without it should be absolutely necessary.

"I think I can bribe and intimidate these Indians into giving up some of the principal murderers," he explained. "And if that can't be done, if force can be got together to warrant the attempt, I would recommend the seizure of some of the chiefs to be held as hostages for the good behavior of tribe."

(It was the first time Sully had suggested the possibility of taking hostages. It would not be the last.)

"As you know," he went on, "it is General Sheridan's wish to make a winter campaign. This will be a very arduous duty for soldiers this winter. I thought that a demand backed by force would perhaps end the matter and prevent the necessity of a winter campaign."

But before Regis deTrobriand could respond, however predictably, events once again intervened, once again unpredictably.

*　　*　　*

On December 13, 1869, a band of Piegan warriors attacked a group of eleven hunters, killing one and wound-ing another seriously. Three days later, the same band attacked and overran a wagon train, stealing thirty prime mules.

68

Seizing the moment, Sully reported the incidents to General Hancock (to whom he had no link in the chain of command) with a familiar comment and suggestion.

"If you are going to strike a blow you have not cavalry enough," he told Hancock in his message of December 17. "It would be well to raise three hundred volunteers."

Hancock took the bait, and the next day forwarded Sully's recommendation to General Sheridan with his intention to implement it.

"I shall recommend that three hundred volunteers (mounted) be immediately called into service for six months," Hancock cabled, "and that General Sully be placed in command of the troops at least for that period.

"It is singular, however...that I have not heard from General deTrobriand," he mused.

Regis deTrobriand had not reported the Piegan raids because he had been visiting Fort Benton and was unaware of them. But if news of the attacks had not yet reached him, word of other developments had.

And as providentially as Alfred Sully's prospects had brightened, they once again faded.

"The whole tribe of Piegans came back sooner than expected," deTrobriand cabled Hancock. "They are divided into several hunting camps along the Marias, with dogs, squaws, and children."

With the return of the Piegans to their winter camps on the Marias River, all things became possible, not for Sully but for Regis deTrobriand. Now too far south of the Medicine Line to escape into British territory when attacked, and obviously unaware that an attack was imminent, the Blackfeet lay within range of deTrobriand and his troops. Their punishment was assured.

And Alfred Sully's last hope was dead.

Little knowing how close Sully had come to success, it

69

was a jubilant Regis deTrobriand who reported to General Hancock on returning to Fort Shaw.

The Piegans, he cabled, "are within easy reach, and I propose to seize the opportunity and strike as soon as we are ready. If the cavalry was at hand I would go at it at once, and the work would be done before New Year's day.

"The camp of Mountain-Chief...I intend to strike first by surprise, killing or capturing those who may be found there.

"I would mention that the weather has become extremely cold, falling to 15° below zero," deTrobriand said. "This change in the weather is not without importance, as it is most likely to keep the Indians wintering on the Marias as long as we may wish them there for our purposes.

"I think this will do," the confident commander concluded, "and that if success attend the expedition no further operations will be necessary to bring the Piegans and others to such terms as the government will think proper."

The path ahead plain, deTrobriand ordered Major Eugene M. Baker, in command of the Second Cavalry at Fort Ellis, and his "entire effective strength" to report to Fort Shaw "with the least possible delay," armed and rationed, and "provided with a good and sufficient supply of medical and surgical stores, for use in the field."

It was Christmas Eve, 1869, and Regis deTrobriand went from his desk to midnight Mass.

Alfred Sully meanwhile, profoundly depressed by the collapse of his vision, prepared to play out his last part in the prelude to the campaign — his meeting with the chiefs of the Blackfeet at their agency on the Teton River.

"It has been snowing and is still, and I do not anticipate a very pleasant trip," he wrote on December 22. "But if I can succeed in getting the chiefs to give up their principal leaders in the late difficulties I will be satisfied no matter what hardships I have to undergo."

As for Regis deTrobriand, his only hope for Sully's mission was that it wouldn't scare off the Indians.

"I had a long talk with him," he reported to Hancock on December 28, "...and he agreed to make his demands to the Indian chiefs without making any military demonstration. This point is very important, as the appearance of a military force at the agency would have no other effect than to scare away the hostiles out of our reach."

He need not have worried.

*   *   *

But if Regis deTrobriand was resolved and Alfred Sully resigned, other people in other places remained in doubt. News of deTrobriand's new-found enthusiasm for the winter campaign had not yet reached General Sheridan in Chicago. He still knew only that for five months no one had seemed able to agree on anything having to do with the Blackfeet.

In August, deTrobriand and Sully had both said the Piegans were at war and both had advised the immediate application of military force. It was the last time they had agreed. A month later, Sully had advocated calling up volunteers while deTrobriand supported the reinforcing of regular troops. Sully had kept up his alarms into October, while deTrobriand appeared by then to have proclaimed peace with the Piegans and declared war on Sully. Later on, Sully was saying one day that he wanted to sit down in council with the friendly chiefs, and the next that he wanted to lead three hundred militiamen against them.

What was going on out there?

Sheridan turned to an old friend and trusted subordinate, Major General James A. Hardie, for the answer.

"It will be seen from the accompanying papers," he wrote Hardie on December 27, "that General deTrobriand and General Sully differ very much in their judgment in reference to Indian affairs in Montana. It appears that General Sully so represented affairs as to cause the Secretary of the Interior to apply to the General-In-Chief for additional protection for the people, and, on this basis, the General authorized me to punish the Piegan Indians, and orders were sent accordingly to General deTrobriand.

"On November 22, General deTrobriand makes a report, from which it will be seen that the reports of Indian depredations are exaggerated; and also, a report of November 26, from which it appears that the condition of Indian affairs is by no means alarming.

"After a careful examination of this correspondence, I desire that you proceed without delay to Montana, and make a thorough examination of the subject."

And finally, Sheridan said, "if there is any danger of Indians being molested who are friendly, you are authorized to suspend all operations."

You have seen something, said Raven. You have seen the sacred hoop. It is the circle of life. Everything is enclosed within it. Everything within it is the same.

...and at all times I prayed, and to all who were of and with Sun.

The-Heavy-Runner's Vision
New Year's Day 1870

AH! I SEE IT today as if it had just been. You cannot
know what it was like then. How happy that far away time.
My mother, filled with life and with pride for her sons. My
father, strong and wise. No sickness in our camps. No
empty bellies. Could all have been so happy? Was there
no sorrow, no pain? Perhaps clouds hide the trouble, and
only light shines through. I do not know.

I had seen twenty summers before I set out upon my
vision quest. Many of my friends had already found secret
helpers. Not I. It had not yet been my time. Not until now,
in the Moon-When-Berries-Ripen of my twenty-first
summer, was it my time. When I told my mother and father
that I would make the quest they were very happy, very
proud. They prayed to all the Above-Ones to help me.
Tears filled my mother's eyes, and she wrapped her beaut-
iful elk robe in a bundle and tied it to a tree as a gift to Sun
for his help. Sun would see it there until it became dust, for

none would dare steal such a sacrifice. My father gave three of his finest ponies to Black-Badger, a sacred man of our village, to make me ready for the quest. The women built a sweat lodge of willow branches.

On the day before my quest was to begin, Black-Badger gathered up his sacred pipe, a wooden bowl of water, and a buffalo tail, and together we entered the sweat lodge, naked. The women heated stones on a fire nearby, and rolled them in to us. Black-Badger dipped the buffalo tail in the bowl and sprinkled water over the stones. Steam so thick we could not see each other rose and filled the lodge. Ah! How hot it was. How the sweat ran from us. I felt all that was bad leave my body. I could have slept, so empty was I. When Black-Badger began to sing it startled me back to myself, alert and wide awake. He sang songs and made prayers to Sun and Night-Light, to Early-Riser and the Seven-Persons, to Thunder and all the Above-Persons, and to all the Ground-Persons and all the Below-Persons, calling on them to pity me and to help me in my quest. Some I had heard many times, but many more were new and strange and filled with power. And I felt a new spirit within me and a new strength, touched by Sun and warmed with his goodness.

When Black-Badger had sung and prayed, we smoked the sacred pipe together. Inside me, in silence, without my calling or asking, my own prayer spoke. It asked for Sun's pity and help. For me and my quest, yes. And for my family — to this day they sit beside me, in my love — for long life and good health. And for my tribe, that they might prosper and know bright days.

Carrying only a pipe and skin of water, I rode the next morning to the fasting place. Six brothers rode with me, to protect me and pray for my success. I had chosen the place long before. It was high in the Sweet Grass Hills, a place of

76

great danger, for many of our dead were buried there and we heard their spirits often, calling to loved ones. When we reached the place, each of my brothers touched my arm and asked Sun to help me, and rode away. I built a small lodge of branches and leaves to keep off the rain. I lay on my right side and waited for Nitsokan.

Two days and nights I lay on my right side, two days and nights on my left side, without covering, eating nothing, drinking only a few sips of water. Beside me was the pipe, ready for my secret helper to smoke when he arrived. And at all times I prayed, and to all who were of and with Sun. To bear I prayed for strength, and to wolf for cunning. To otter for success on the hunt I prayed, and to eagle for courage and long life. Take pity on me, I prayed to Sun and his helpers. Help me with your power. And to Earth I prayed, mother of all, to nourish and protect me, her son.

On the fourth night Sun took pity on me.

Early-Riser rode high in the sky when my shadow departed. Into the night sky I soared. Below me I saw the small, rough lodge in the Sweet Grass Hills where my body lay. Smaller and more indistinct it grew as my spirit floated higher and higher. I was without weight or thought, all cords to Earth cut through, alone in the darkness. How long I flew alone I cannot tell, and might never have known had not a voice spoken to me.

Of all Above-Ones, whose eyes are most sharp? the voice asked. And I answered, Raven.

Who of all flyers brings news from far off? the voice asked. Again I answered, Raven.

It is true, the voice said, and took shape before me. It was Raven, flying with me.

Have you come to be my helper, I asked, to share with me your power?

None escape my eyes, he said. However deep in the

77

forest, nothing hides from my sight. However far off on the prairie, I see the smallest one.

Have you come to be my helper? I asked once more, to share with me your power?

From other ones come other powers, Raven said. To be strong. To be wise. To cure sickness. To find food always. To bring good weather. To defeat your enemies. These are the powers of others. From them must you find such help.

Have you no power? I asked him.

Of all powers, he answered, mine is greatest. Without it we are nothing.

Will you share your power with me? I asked.

I will, he said. But first you must ask my help, and swear to use the power I give you always. Do you ask? Do you swear?

I do, I told him. Pity me, help me. I ask your help. I need your power, and swear to use it always.

It is good, he said. I will help you.

We flew together in darkness and silence until I could hold back the words no longer. What power will you give me? I asked.

And he answered, the power to see.

My heart grew big with joy. Ah! Ah! Was I not of all men most fortunate. In my heart I gave thanks to Sun for opening his hand to me.

On we flew together in darkness until once more the words would not be contained. How will I see, I asked, and what, when all around is darkness?

Are we far from your camp? he asked in turn.

Yes, I said. Many sleeps.

He gave me then his medicine, and told me to rub it into my eyes. As I did, the lodges of my band — my mother's and father's, Black-Badger's, all — appeared to my eyes, so close I seemed to be among them. I saw the people sitting around their campfires, talking softly, the children at play, the women cooking and sewing, horses and dogs resting. The men smoked, and I saw them smile and heard them sometimes laugh.

What do you see? Raven asked.

I said, My people. And we flew on.

Soon another camp came into my eyes. I saw it was a band of Blue-Paint People, gathered around their campfires, smoking and cooking and talking, their children at play, their animals at rest. Often the people smiled, and laughed sometimes, too.

What do you see? Raven asked.

I said, Blue-Paint People. And we flew on.

To camp after camp of us Lone People of the plains we flew, to camps of the Cutthroats and the Liars, the Parted-Hairs and the Spotted-Horses, camp after camp. At each I saw the people at their campfires, praying, working, resting, playing. At each, Raven asked what I saw. At each I answered with the name of that people. And we flew on.

We flew at last to a village of the Many-Bracelets in Always-Summer land. Their lodges were not of hides but of earth and they grew their food in fields instead of hunting buffalo. And still as in our own camps they sat about their fires, the sound of talk and laughter, of work and of play, rising with the smoke.

What do you see? Raven asked.

A village of the Many-Bracelets, I said. A village not like ours, but a people like our Black-Footed People.

You have seen something, said Raven. All Lone People have the same face.

And we flew on.

To the rising Sun we flew, to the All-Over-Water, where

at last we saw a place of many-houses. There was no prairie, no mountains, no forest. Only houses. Houses large and small, made of wood and stone. Some high as hills. And Napikwan. Ah! More white-skinned ones than trees, as many as stars. And I saw into their houses, saw them gathered before their fires. I heard their voices, heard their laughter. Saw them at work, cooking and sewing and building from wood. Watched the games of their children. Saw their animals feeding and resting.

And Raven asked, What do you see?

I see Napikwan, I said, and his face too is the same.

You have seen something, said Raven. All are sons and daughters of the Earth, our mother.

And we flew on.

Below us were no people. Only the ground, the rivers and lakes. Four-foots fed and slept and ran, white-horns and big-ears, long-tails and wood-biters. Deep in the water lay the swimmers that cannot be eaten. Above us, flyers soared and dived. And over all the ground, the grasses and plants and trees growing there.

What do you see? asked Raven.

I see Earth, our mother, I answered, with all her sons and daughters, in all their faces.

You have seen something, said Raven. The ground has mercy for all. At her breast all living things, with legs or wings or fins or roots, are little children nursing.

And we flew on.

Up the sacred Wolves Trail we flew, beyond our world, into the stars. Through Thunder we flew to the edge of the sky. Behind us lay the days when the Black-Footed People made arrow points from stone, when we had only dogs to move camp. Ahead stretched the Sand Hills and beyond, to the jumping-off place, and the shadows of those gone before and the spirits of those to come danced and sang.

And Raven asked, What do you see?

I see that all Earth's children are one with all who have been or will be, I answered.

You have seen something, said Raven. You have seen the sacred hoop. It is the circle of life. Everything is enclosed within it. Everything within it is the same.

Shadow and bird, we returned to the Sweet Grass Hills and my place of fasting. There Raven departed. I watched his dark wings, heard his powerful words.

Keep the sacred hoop, he called, and all directions lead to home.

When I returned to camp I held my first feast-and-smoke. We smoked four pipes.

*   *   *

It was late in the afternoon of New Year's day, 1870, when Alfred Sully arrived at the Blackfeet agency on the Teton River. He had sent a messenger into the winter encampments of Bloods and Piegans to notify the chiefs of his wish to meet with them, and had anticipated that a majority — perhaps twelve or fifteen in all — would comply. But they did not. Only Big-Lake, Little-Wolf, and The-Heavy-Runner among the Piegan leaders, and Grey-Eyes alone of all the Blood chiefs responded.

"I was disappointed in not meeting more," Sully wrote later, "but when my messenger reached the camp, he found the Indians very much intoxicated, and some of the headmen so much overcome that it was impossible for them to meet me.

"This has been their frequent condition," he continued, "and there appears to be no means of stopping this evil."

Though discouraged, Sully presented his demands.

Owl-Child and the others accused of the murder of

Four-Bears must be captured and delivered up for trial. All stolen horses and mules must be returned. All raids must end and the good behavior of the young warriors guaranteed.

If the demands were met, he told the chiefs, there could be peace and friendship between whites and Blackfeet. If they were not, there would be war.

And, Sully warned, if there were war, the Northern-White-Men had agreed to permit seizers to pursue the Blackfeet across the Medicine Line.

There would be no refuge, no escape.

Speaking for the chiefs, The-Heavy-Runner asked first for food and blankets. The winter had been hard and the hunting bad, he told Sully. His people were cold and hungry.

Sully replied that there could be no help until the demands were met.

How strange for it to come to this, thought The-Heavy-Runner. How strange that all lives should hang on revenge for the death of Four-Bears. How strange that whites and Blackfeet should both wish justice for the renegade Owl-Child, the outcast who cannot tell friend from enemy, who murders clansman and brother. How strange that on this, on this unnatural quarrel which began so long ago and will not end, on this should hang life or death for the Black-Footed People.

He spoke of the difficulties in capturing Owl-Child and the other fugitives alive.

They will be as hard to find as white-big-head, who lives among the high rocks and ledges of the Backbone, he said, or mountain-devil, who leaves tracks but is never seen. Owl-Child is sometimes here and sometimes there and then is gone. No one knows where he goes or for what reason. He is hated by many, and he has learned to run and hide and fight like the four-foots. He has been too much pursued to be captured. He knows the signs. He will not be trapped alive. If he is to be punished, it will be necessary to kill him. Only this is possible.

Sully agreed.

The stolen horses and mules, too, will be difficult to track, The-Heavy-Runner continued, and still more difficult to take from those who now keep them, and return to you. But I believe this much is possible, and I promise we will try.

But we have lost control of our young men, he told Sully. The sneaking-drink-givers madden them with rum and set fire to their spirits. That is why they steal and kill. They will not listen to us. We can do nothing.

Sully could say no more. It was done. Big-Lake, Little-Wolf, and Grey-Eyes signed their approval. The-Heavy-Runner asked Alfred Sully for a sign of their agreement.

It is the strongest wish of my life that all children of the Great Father live together in friendship, he said. What I ask is a paper which says that we are friends, a sign which shows that The-Heavy-Runner is friend to the whites.

Sully agreed to prepare the document, and for Big-Lake, Little-Wolf and Grey-Eyes also. A pipe was passed, and Alfred Sully parted from the four old chiefs.

"I hope my mission to the Piegans and Bloods may be a success," he wrote on January 3, 1870, "yet I am not oversanguine. Two or three weeks will determine. In the meantime I would recommend the commander of the District not to retard any preparations he may contemplate, so that he may be ready to strike, if necessary, should it prove that these chiefs cannot carry out their good intentions with their own people."

He need not have worried about Regis deTrobriand

delaying on his account.

"He met with some of their chiefs," reported deTrobriand to General Hancock, also on January 3, "and got
nothing but words."

"Within ten days," he wrote, "the winter drill."

If the lives and property of citizens of Montana can best be protected by striking Mountain-Chief's band of Piegans, I want them struck. Tell Baker to strike them HARD.

Orders of
Lt. Gen. Philip H. Sheridan
January 15, 1870

Piegan

General Hardie's Report
January 7 to 15, 1870

T HE REPORT OF Inspector General James A. Hardie to Lieutenant General Philip H. Sheridan on the status of Indian Affairs in Montana:

1870

Upon reaching Montana [on January 7, 1980], I found that the wide-spread alarm excited during the past summer by the depredations of the Blackfeet had yielded to a calmer and more accurate view of the situation.

In times of Indian disturbances, the alarm caused by Indian raids naturally leads to the circulation of inaccurate and frequently wild reports, and in a period of excitement, the public danger is apt to be magnified by parties whose interests lie in the promotion of military schemes that will cause the disbursement of money or will furnish employment for the otherwise idle. Especially might this be the case where the business affairs of a community are unprosperous, as have been the trade and the mining interests of Montana for the last two years. I have no doubt that there had been some alarm that was unnecessary and some that was simulated. But for all that, events have actually occurred which were of such consequence as to produce much exasperation and genuine and well-grounded solicitude among the people.

In Montana, as in most of our other Territories where there are Indians, there are two classes of people. One is that of the citizen interested in the settlement and civilization of the country; the other connected with the Indians in some way, either through trade or inter-marriage, or belonging to the Indian service. The former class is naturally timid as respects Indian disturbances. With their experience and knowledge of the Indian character they dread their savage neighbor. They know they are the natural objects of their enmity; they have families, homes and fortune, all exposed to their inroads; they have been witnesses of their horrible butcheries, their brutalities to women, their mad ferocity in dealing with those falling into their power. The complete subjection of Indians is absolutely essential to their sense of security. The other class have generally not so much to fear. They do not, as do the settlers, encroach on the Indians' lands. The traders are their friends. Besides, the traders whose business would be broken up by military operations (if they be personally safe) would be loth to admit a condition of things calling for such operations. This class leans toward the Indians, and would be apt to resist belief of evil disposition on their part.

Then there are unprincipled and unscrupulous men of all classes who speak and act without reference to the truth and right, in pursuit of their private ends or the gratification of their passions.

The troops do not court Indian campaigns. They are in a position to estimate more nearly the real danger. They would be naturally inclined to turn a deaf ear to clamor and to be deliberate in their judgments.

From this diversity of position, of interests, and of feeling, naturally flow differences in opinion and different

88

views of facts, always likely to be intensified by controversy. Hence the necessity of discovering the sources of reports in order to ascertain the real truth in any question.

It is not deemed necessary to make a particular application of the foregoing to the clearing up of the discrepancies exhibited in the correspondence. The sequel will show such a concurrence of testimony as to leave little room for doubt.

Additional aggressions (December 13 and 17) appear to have assisted to modify the views of General deTrobriand as to the gravity of the situation, and to have so impressed General Sully, that he suggested raising three hundred volunteers and, indeed, proposed to command an expedition himself. These aggressions deepened the solicitude of the community, but the knowledge that military preparations were on foot gave expectation of relief.

Much of the trouble General Sully attributes to the prevalence of drunkenness among the Indians, and he earnestly pressed the use of troops to break up the whisky trade. General Sully thought that the need to replace horses sold for liquor frequently incited the Indians to steal. There is, no doubt, truth in this; but the facilities for running stock across the line and for trading it advantageously with bands on that side, and perhaps on the Hudson Bay posts, are so great, and the ease and impunity with which such raids could be made so well understood, that to minds excited and reckless from drunkenness, the temptation to plunder the settlements is irresistible. It seems impracticable to prevent this by use of troops.

The prevention of the sale of whisky to Indians has not hitherto seemed a possibility. The reservation of these Indians has never been confirmed. There is no certainty as to its being Indian Territory within the meaning of the law prohibiting sales of whiskey to Indians. But the trade is conducted so secretly that it would be difficult to stop it if the power to arrest traders and destroy their liquor were unquestioned.

The smallpox prevailed to considerable extent among the Indians, and is thought by some to have had the effect to intensify hostility of many of the Blackfeet against the whites, to whom they attribute the introduction among them of the disease.

On the 6th of December, General Sully telegraphed that he proposed visiting the Blackfeet to demand the murderers and stolen property. It appears that General deTrobriand entertained no hopes of the success of General Sully's scheme. On reaching Fort Shaw, I found that General deTrobriand's views, respecting the necessity for chastisement of the Piegans and proper time for the blow, had apparently undergone modification. I therefore addressed him a note inquiring if such were the case.

FROM: Hardie   Fort Shaw
TO: deTrobriand   January 11

Your reports of September 9 and November 26 set forth generally that the condition of Indian affairs on this frontier was not then alarming; that although certain depredations had been committed by small parties of neighboring tribes of Indians, their number and import had been exaggerated, and that the main body have had nothing to do with these attacks, the responsibility of which rests upon a small band of Piegans. If events have occurred to modify the conclusions of those reports, will you be good enough to inform me what they are, and what are your present views?

He replied that since November 26 events had occurred which materially altered the condition of things.

FROM: deTrobriand   Fort Shaw
TO: Hardie   January 13

The first of these is the return of the Indians (Piegans and Bloods) on the Marias River about the middle of December, when they were not expected to come there before the end of January. This created an opportunity for striking the Piegans at once, which did not exist before.

In the meantime, General Sully proposed to make a demand on the Indians for the delivery of the murderers and the recovery of animals stolen. This demand was to be backed by a military force, the plan being approved. This had the effect of paralyzing any independent action on my part by putting the military forces of my command virtually at the disposal of the superintendent of Indian affairs in Montana. As this was, in my opinion, calculated to defeat the success of the contemplated expedition by giving alarm to the Indians, I attempted to obtain a prevention of the interference of General Sully, but without success, and General Sully arrived at Fort Shaw on December 25. What took place in his council with *four* Indian chiefs is stated in his report. I do not think it necessary to add anything.

To come back to the object of your communication: the other events which took place to alter the condition of affairs during the month of December are:

1. An attack on a party of hunters at the head of Sun River Valley on December 13, in which one man was killed and another wounded by a band of Piegans.

2. The loss of a herd of thirty mules belonging to Mr. Kirkendall, stolen December 16 near Dearborn by the same band of Piegans, and not Blackfeet, as erroneously reported by General Sully.

3. The breaking open of a log house and stealing or destroying the provisions contained therein, near Camp Cooke; the pursuit of the marauders, and the fight which lasted several hours without result. This on the evening of

91

the 22nd and during the 23rd of December.

These three attacks, without any sort of provocation whatever, and occurring almost simultaneously and immediately upon the arrival of the Indians on the Marias, show in what disposition they have returned, and how prompt they are to resume their murderous and plundering incursions, unfortunately unchecked during the past summer for want of means of repression. It is my firm belief that they are greatly encouraged by their past impunity, and that it has become necessary to inflict a punishment on the guilty parties, mostly Piegans. This not only to chastise the culprits, but as a warning to prevent others.

This does not imply that my views are changed respecting the general disposition of the Blackfeet nation. It is still my opinion that no state of war actually exists, and that the majority of the Indians are peacefully disposed. But among them all, and principally among the Piegans, there is a certain number of ill-disposed and positively hostile young men which must be punished, as they cannot be controlled by the friendly chiefs, and are even openly sustained by other chiefs, the most conspicuous of whom are Mountain-Chief and his sons. These we must strike, and strike hard, so as to make an example.

So far as the striking goes (provided the action of General Sully does not scare them away), I can do it with the forces now at my command. I would cut the line of the Marias so as to leave out the Bloods, limiting the punishment to the Piegans. And even among them I would be careful that two friendly bands of The-Heavy-Runner and Big-Lake be left unmolested, so as to single out Mountain-Chief and his followers, who were, two days ago, still at the place known as the Big Bend. This, successfully accomplished, would not, according to all probabilities short of a certainty, bring any general war. Still, every possible contingency must be taken into consideration. Therefore, in case of an extensive war, and serious hostilities in the spring, I shall need re-enforcements, principally cavalry, to carry it forward with vigor and effect.

General Sully's conference with the Indians took place on the 1st. I had not expected any efficacious result from this conference; it was a failure at the start. General Sully himself, indeed, was not sanguine of any success. General deTrobriand, as I have said, thought nothing would come of it. But this much was done; the Indians were distinctly informed that "the government was tired out with the repeated aggressions of their people," and had "determined to make war against them" if they did not furnish the guarantee of future good conduct. They agreed to effect the restitution of all the stolen stock they could get, and to try and have the murderers killed.

To verify accounts and to get fresh information on what progress was being made by the Indians to carry into effect their promises, I caused a messenger to be sent to the Marias. This messenger, who knew the Indians well, whom I had heard generally well spoken of, and who had the confidence of General deTrobriand, left Fort Shaw January 8 and returned January 12. From what the messenger saw and heard, it was clear that the Indians did not seem to be earnestly trying to effect anything toward the fulfillment of their promises. They had talked about doing something. But though there was stolen stock (some he saw and recognized) distributed through the different bands, both the Bloods and Piegans, there was no effort to get it and bring it in. Among the Indians he saw were Little-Wolf and The-Heavy-Runner. Little-Wolf said that General Sully demanded Owl-Child, Star and Crow-Top, all concerned in murders. Owl-Child is the only one there. He said he could not give them up alive, as they might kill him; yet if Owl-Child were killed no one would care, as he is a sort of renegade. He was with the Bloods when the messenger was there.

The messenger learned among the Bloods that they

thought they were not going to be molested by the troops but they believed the Piegans would be punished, or those of the Piegans who had committed crimes. The Bloods, therefore, seemed indifferent to the matter. This differs from what the Indians told General Sully, where they claimed that the South Piegans were innocent as well as the Bloods, thus throwing all the blame on the Indians not so generally ranging south of the line.

The messenger gave the localities of the particular encampments of Mountain-Chief, Bear-Chief, and other bands of Piegans, both those called friendly and unfriendly, and, what was important, informed me that if sent with any expedition against the Piegans — and it was designed to send him — he thought he could distinguish the marauding bands it was contemplated to strike from those not intended to be punished upon seeing the Indians, and could inform the commanding officer. His statements were sufficiently confirmed by other testimony to entitle them to credit.

On the 10th of January I telegraphed to General Sully to direct Lieutenant Pease, agent of the Blackfeet, to meet me at Fort Shaw. He reached Fort Shaw on the 13th. He informed me that not having been long agent of the Blackfeet — he was appointed last summer — he had no intimate knowledge of their affairs. The criminal acts which had been committed, he thought, were chargeable principally to the Piegans. He had no information as to anything being done by the Indians toward securing murderers or stolen stock. He attributed a great deal of trouble to an abundance of whiskey among the Indians.

On the 10th of January I telegraphed to General Sully:

FROM: Hardie   Fort Shaw
TO: Sully   January 10

I would be glad to know what definite period you fix as that
beyond which you will wait no further for the compliance
of Indians with their promises to bring in property, etc.

FROM: Sully   Helena
TO: Hardie   January 10

Two weeks is the time I thought necessary to give the
Indians.

On the 11th, General Sully wrote me that he had telegraphed to Mr. Eastman, in charge of the Northwest Fur
Company, at Fort Benton, to ascertain if he knew of
anything being done toward the recovery of stolen stock,
etc. Mr. Eastman replied that "he had heard nothing." He
added in a note to General Sully, dated the 13th of
January, as follows:

> It has been reported to me that Big-Leg said while here
> that he was going to leave his tribe; that he had talked with
> them about going to war, and they would not listen. It is my
> opinion that the Indians will do nothing, either regarding
> stolen stock or capturing these men. These men who are
> running back and forth from the camps tell them the whites
> won't fight; and Mr. Reiplinger tells me that the only thing
> you can't make them believe is that the whites will fight. I
> have seen another party who says that Big-Leg told him
> that he was going to bring part of his band into the agency;
> that he would not fight the whites; and that his young men
> would not listen to him.

General Sully also said in his note that he thought "it
would be a good thing to give those Piegans a scare,
particularly the Mountain-Chief's band;" although he
feared that such was the ease with which the reports of

95

movements would be carried to the Indians, through half-breeds and whiskey-sellers, that our troops would find no Indians south of the line.

FROM Hardie   Fort Shaw
TO: Sully   January 13

Your letter received. Messenger sent to the Marias and the agency returned last night. No serious efforts among Piegans generally to comply with promise to you. Little-Wolf has sent two boys to Belly River for mules. Mountain-Chief and others doing nothing. No great hope. Mountain-Chief camped separately from Bloods. Two weeks up tomorrow. What do you say as to the best policy now? You know the situation. Reply by telegraph.

FROM: Sully   Helena
TO: Hardie   January 13

Under the circumstances, as you telegraph, I would, if possible, capture Mountain-Chief and some of his principal men and hold them as hostages until the nation fulfill their promise to me.

General Sully wrote me to the same effect, but more at length:

FROM: Sully   Helena
TO: Hardie   January 13

I have received your telegraph and have answered it. I am still of the same opinion in regard to a campaign against the Blackfeet: that the parties most deserving punishment will not receive their just rewards without a force can cross the frontier; and until this can be done, no permanent good will result from any movement of troops. However, as some of the most active members of the late marauding parties did belong to Mountain-Chief's band, although it is said these individual Indians are at present north of the line, it would be well to show them we are in earnest, and the seizure of old Mountain-Chief and about half a dozen other principal men of his band would, I think, cause the rest to go after the stolen animals. It will be a difficult matter to make any movement without the Indians getting information. Would it not be well, therefore, to give it out when the move is made, that the troops are started to cross the line to recapture stolen stock; that permission has been given our government to do so. Then, after the troops have passed the Marias, to double on the track at night, so as to reach Mountain-Chief's camp by daylight. But whatever is done, precaution should be taken to give Mr. Reiplinger and his trading-party military protection. After any move is made they will very likely be massacred, and all their very valuable stock of goods destroyed. I also gave a wagon-master of Mr. Kirkendall permission to go north with the Indians, to see if he could get back some of the mules stolen lately. For these reasons I would recommend that for the present no blood should be shed, if it is possible to avoid it.

I was quite unprepared for this recommendation, in view of the opinions and recommendations of General Sully up to the 13th of January. His report of January 3 recommends "not to retard any preparation he may contemplate, so that he may be ready to strike." His reports procured the issuing of an order from the War Department for military action. He thought considerable additions should be made to the troops. He had contemplated to conduct the operations himself. Before final measures were taken, he had resorted to negotiations; that had failed. The necessary inference was that the time had come to "strike" as contemplated.

The experience and character of General Sully, as well as his official position, lent to his recommendation due weight in my mind; but I could not feel the measure he now proposed would fully meet the case.

It certainly was very desirable that blood should not be shed if it were possible to avoid it. But then there is the duty of providing security for the lives and property of the citizens of Montana, and that is imperious. To shrink from doing what the occasion called for as necessary, no matter how severe, is to incur responsibility for future massacres of men, women, and children, for the destruction of homes and the plunder and ruin of the settlements. What did the occasion call for as necessary? To this General deTrobriand had answered: A sharp and severe blow upon some guilty bands as an example to the rest.

A view of the situation seemed to me to justify his opinion.

The inhabitants of Montana had, in truth, suffered much. The aggressors were perfectly uncontrollable by the Indian Department, which had especially called for the assistance of the military. Their incursions had been repeated over and over again. Things were getting worse, and in fact war parties were actually out at this time. It was the universal belief among the citizens and military that there was no hope unless the strong arm of the government made itself felt upon them. The authorized trade among them even thought so. Warnings and negotiations had failed. They could not be made to believe that the whites would fight them. Some of the offending bands were now within reach. No doubt the Blackfeet north of the line had done mischief, and their safety gave them impunity and therefore encouragement. But the object is to stop aggressions for the future, not to punish for the past. A single blow on any guilty band would be probably efficacious as more extended operations. Such a plan certainly would be more sparing of blood and better on all accounts than a war.

To attempt to surprise an Indian band and capture prisoners without bloodshed would be ordinarily to attempt an impracticability. A combat and consequent loss of life would be inevitable, or else there would be the flight of the Indians and total failure — a worse condition of things than if no operations had been undertaken all. This form of coercion would be totally ineffectual even if the hostages could be obtained, without some measure of punishment. These marauders were indifferent and reckless, shuffling off their guilt upon others when accused; under no control from the older men; pretending peace when they meant plunder and murder, and were satisfied of their impunity. Failure to punish them as threatened would have been badly construed and have strengthened their sense of impunity.

The disposition of these Indians toward the whites is doubtful, varying from indifference to hostility. It is, in my judgment, extremely improbable that they will adopt reservation life. These Indians are well armed and provided with ammunition. The Bloods are generally peacefully disposed. The Blackfeet north of the line are either indifferent or hostile. The Piegans are mostly inclined to hostility. The chiefs known to be friendly are The-Heavy-Runner, Big-Lake (or Leg), Little-Wolf, and The-Boy; the others are doubtful or positively hostile. Among the latter class are Mountain-Chief and his two sons, the elder of whom shot young Clarke; Owl-Child (full Indian, but speaks English), the murderer of Clarke; Star, a half Mexican and half Piegan, a noted murderer; Crow-Top, a noted murderer; the Cut-Hand; Eagle's-Rib (one of the party that murdered Mr. Clarke), Bear-Chief (of the party that murdered Clarke), Under-Bull, Red-Horn, Bull's Head, The-White-Man's-Dog, and The-Black-Weasel (of the party that murdered Clarke).

The facts and considerations presented in the foregoing pages I reported in brief to the Lieutenant General by telegraph, asking for his instructions:

FROM: Hardie   Fort Shaw
TO: Sheridan   January 13

Condition of Indian affairs not alarming, but depredations
have been repeated and a man killed. Public excitement
not great, but military action a necessity. deTrobriand
thinks impunity encourages Indians, and recommends
prompt chastisement. Sully found most chiefs too drunk to
meet him. The chiefs promised to try to get stock, though
not to bring in men, but to have them killed; two weeks
given. Time really up tomorrow. I sent messenger north.
Indians there and not far from here. Messenger returned
last night. Reports feeble efforts only are made for recovery of stock. Pretense of desire for peace and to try to get
stock, but there is no great hope of success. Much stock in
British possessions. Young and hostile cannot be controlled by old and more friendly. The Bloods do not expect
punishment, but expect troops to punish bad Piegans.
Bloods and Piegans camped along the Marias now.
Mountain-Chief's band small, but great rascals, encamped
separately. deTrobriand thinks he can strike them without
molesting friends, either Piegans or Bloods. There is
reasonable ground for his opinion, but he wishes to chastise.

Sully is more moderate, and now advises that
Mountain-Chief's band be captured and held as hostages
until nation fulfills promises to him.

I have not interfered with military arrangements. The
Cavalry will reach here tomorrow from Fort Ellis. It will not
be ready for movement before Sunday or Monday. It will
endeavor to surprise camp. I fear information will reach
Indians, but trial should be had. Of course, British line will
not be crossed.

Question is, whether chastisement or capture for hostages
should be principal design. Practical result of movement, a
simple one; result would probably be killing and capturing,
both.

100

Under all circumstances, how far should the opinion of General Sully as to scope of operations govern the military?

I think the military commander (Colonel Baker) should be allowed to proceed generally according to circumstances under which he finds himself in his operations, having in view securing the fulfillment of promises, etc., and the best interests of the frontier.

The Lieutenant General telegraphed me as follows:

FROM: Sheridan   Chicago
TO: Hardie   January 15

If the lives and property of citizens of Montana can best be protected by striking Mountain-Chief's band of Piegans, I want them struck. Tell Baker to strike them HARD.

On the 15th of January I had an interview with Colonel Baker, who had reached Fort Shaw. I communicated to that officer and to General deTrobriand the instructions contained in the Lieutenant General's telegram; I requested that the safety of Mr. Reiplinger and his trading post might be provided for.

I learned that it was the design of General deTrobriand to send as guide with Colonel Baker the messenger whom I had dispatched to the Marias. Young Clarke had also volunteered to go as guide in order to avenge the murder of his father. Thus certainty was secured as far as possible that no friendly Indians would be molested.

Following is the text of instructions given to Colonel Baker:

FROM: deTrobriand   Fort Shaw
TO: Baker   January 16

You will proceed with your command, without any more delay than may be required by the present condition of the weather, to chastise that portion of the Indian tribe of Piegans which, under Mountain-Chief or his sons, com-

101

mitted the greater part of the murders and depredations of last summer and last month in this district.

The band of Mountain-Chief is now encamped on the Marias River, at a place called the Big Bend, and can be easily singled out from other bands of Piegans, two of which should be left unmolested, as they have uniformly remained friendly, viz., the bands of The-Heavy-Runner and Big-Lake.

All the Piegans now on the territory of the United States are encamped along the Marias River, from the trading post near the Red Coulee down to near the mouth of the river, and this section, up to the frontier line, will be the field of your operations.

Above the trading post is encamped about one-half of the Bloods. They should be left alone. The Blackfeet proper, being far away in the British possessions and not considered as hostile, will not come in your way.

All necessary information in regard to the location of the several encampments and the character of the roaming Indians who may fall in your hands during your operations will be furnished you by the guide who is ordered to report to you.

When you strike the Marias River, or at such a time when it may not any more convey a premature information, you will leave or send a small detachment of ten men to the trading post of the Northwest Fur Company for the protection of the establishment during your operations.

Beyond these general instructions it is deemed unnecessary to add anything. The details as to the best way to surprise the enemy and to carry on successfully the operations are confidently left to your judgment and discretion, according to circumstances and to your experience in such expeditions.

I telegraphed to the headquarters of the division as follows:

FROM: Hardie   Helena
TO: Sheridan   January 17

Reached here last night from Fort Shaw. The Lieutenant
General's telegram of the 15th received. I think chastisement necessary. In this Colonel Baker concurs. He knew
the General's wishes. He will move today. Some horses
and mules stolen from citizens in various Indian camps on
the Marias, among them camps of Indians pretending to
be innocent.

Also murderers there. The stock the Indians promised
Sully to deliver up; the latter to have been killed. I thought
it well Colonel Baker's design should be extended to
include the coercion of Indians to keep this promise, if he
could do so prudently. Hence my suggestion at close of
long dispatch. But this is only following up of stroke directed by Lieutenant General, and Colonel Baker may be
relied on to do all that the General would wish in the way of
vigorous and sufficient action. If Indians do not get wind of
movement, and the weather has been opportunely severe
to prevent measureably that danger, I anticipate best results. In any case good, and no harm, will be done.

The deed is done. The murder of Malcolm Clarke has been avenged; the guilty Indians have been punished.

Helena Daily Herald
February 2, 1870

I saw The-Heavy-Runner come from his painted lodge. He carried the paper our Father had given him. He called out to the seizers as he walked. "I am The-Heavy-Runner, friend to the whites. Do not shoot us."

Black-Antelope

It was pursue or perish.

Death For The-Heavy-Runner
January 23, 1870

THAT THE CHASTISEMENT of the Piegans could now commence came as no surprise to readers of the *Helena Daily Herald,* who as early as January 12, 1870, had been alerted to the impending attack. "We are informed that the four companies of cavalry under command of Col. Baker, which passed the town yesterday evening enroute to Fort Shaw, are proceeding thither to engage in active service," the paper reported.

Colonel Eugene M. Baker arrived at Fort Shaw on January 14, intending to start immediately the march for the Marias. Temperatures, however, fell to 43 degrees below zero, and the expedition was delayed by the fierce cold.

There were nearly 350 men in Baker's force, including ten officers and 207 enlisted men of Companies F, G, H, and L of the Second United States Cavalry, and 55 mounted infantrymen and 75 foot soldiers of the Thirteenth United States Infantry. With them also were the now recovered Horace Clarke, sworn to avenge the murder of his father and his own shooting, and Joseph Kipp, known to the Blackfeet as Raven-Quiver. Kipp was the mixed-blood Piegan son of an early American Fur Company trader, and the messenger to whom Inspector General Hardie had referred in his report, now serving as Baker's scout charged with responsibility, as Hardie had described it, to "distinguish the marauding bands it was contemplated to strike from those not intended to be punished."

As everyone knew, that was the problem: how to tell friend from enemy when all have the same face.

On January 13, in the original draft of a letter to Hardie, Regis deTrobriand recognized the problem, wrote of it, but chose to delete it from the final version.

"If we can surprise and punish isolately the band of Mountain-Chief, kill Owl-Child and a few other notorious murderers, the end will be attained, I think, without further danger," he had written. "But if innocent and friendly parties happen to be involved in the chastisement, it may be that the effect will be quite different.

"There lies the difficulty — that is, how to discriminate in the field among the Indians when our men come upon them if they happen to be intermixed around the trading post and on the banks of the Marias, as is the case now.

"Of course," deTrobriand had added, "no effort will be neglected towards that discrimination; but who can say how successfully?"

Who indeed.

"From the extensive preparations that are being made," reported the Herald on January 16, "it is evident that something of more than ordinary moment is contemplated. The general, and I may say universal, opinion is, that the murderers of Clarke are doomed."

*　　*　　*

Cold-Maker comes early to the Ground-Of-Many-Gifts. Later he howls and rages, shrouding the gentle cottonwoods, burying the sweet timothy and bright weasel-eyed berries. But early, before the Wind-Moon swallows itself, Cold-Maker comes in secret silence, more sensed than seen, chilling the lengthening darkness with his breath, his hand stilling, slowing its heavy summer pulse.

On such nights Blackfeet women stirred in their sleep, restless within their dark thickets of fur, and heard there was no wind and saw there was no shadow, and knew that Cold-Maker had once more come to live among them.

And the next day they spoke quietly to their men of moving to winter camp.

If Sun had favored the summer hunt, winter was an easy season for the people beneath the Backbone, and the winter camp a joyful and a pleasing place for body and spirit.

From Sun's favor came abundant meat, and the camp knew no hunger. Parfleches were swollen with pemmican and dried flesh of the buffalo-brother, his tongue and backfat, his boss ribs and his brain. The bellies of women and warriors, of ancient and of infants, all were filled. And all were content.

From Sun's favor, too, came the reuniting of the bands, sound and healthy, emerged without casualty from the dangers of the hunt, with no empty places around the council fires. Following the summer encampment, the all-consuming celebration of Sun, the many bands of the Blackfeet sought out their separate paths in pursuit of the buffalo herds, each to the hunting grounds of its fathers and its chiefs. But with the coming of Cold-Maker, the bands recombined into wintering communities, larger and more social than the hunting brigades. Lone-Fighters welcomed brother-friends from among the Never-Laughs

109

band. Black-Patched-Moccasins raised their painted lodges side by side with Fat-Melters and Skunks. Many-Medicines and Hard-Topknots warmed themselves before common lodgefires. For many days and nights the new-forming assemblies echoed with the glad sounds of recognition and reunion.

And from Sun's summer favor came that most profound of winter pleasures — rest, respite from the wanderings of their nomadic nation. The winter camp was an island to the Black-Footed-People in their restless ocean of grass, an oasis in the endlessly shifting northern desert which was their home. It was a moment of permanence, an instant of settlement in an eternity of movement. To this people ever on the wing, the winter encampment was a time for the building of nests.

The bands selected winter camp sites which offered flat ground for the lodges, clear drinking water, wood for fires, pasture for horses, and shelter from wind and snow — requirements met rarely except in a river valley or bottom, and most often at a sharp bend in the stream. There, high, natural cliffs along the river provided necessary protection from the elements. Cottonwoods growing in the flat bulge created by the river bend added further shelter, besides providing browse for horses and attracting deer, elk and other winter game. In such places the bands of the Black-feet Nation spent the long winter moons in the unique melding of industry and indolence, of playfulness and prayer, which distinguished the Indian way of life from that of all societies before or since.

When Sun had looked with favor upon the summer hunt, it was a good time, a time to make weapons, and medicine, and love. A time to smoke, to hunt for the joy of the hunt, and to be happy.

The children spun their carved wooden tops on the ice

110

and flew down the river banks on sleds with buffalo-rib runners. And their laughter joined that of their fathers, sliding their spear-like snake sticks along the ice in contests of distance and accuracy, and of their mothers, gambling at dice or concealing small bones in the hand game of rhythm and deception.

Warm within their lodges, comfortable and content, the Black-Footed-People passed the winter in ease and pleasure upon the Ground-Of-Many-Gifts, working and gambling, dancing and praying, wondering and dreaming, and recounting the magical, powerful night tales which if told by day would rob a man's eyes of sight.

When Sun had looked with favor upon the summer hunt.

But if Sun had withheld his favor from the summer hunters, had forced them to hunt alone, unguided by his knowledge of where the buffalo grazed, and unaided by his power over their wanderings, then the winter camp was a place not of pleasure but of pain, not of plenty but of starvation, not of warmth but of terrible, killing cold. In such a camp no songs were heard, no laughter, no shouts of greeting. None gambled. None danced. No children spun tops on the river ice or flew on rib-runnered sleds. In such a camp there was no time for games. All hunted, driven by hunger and desperation. For the parfleches lay empty, and survival hung each day on the shooting of a rabbit or the snaring of a sage hen. Children contested with warriors for the meager prey, which was soon exhausted or driven far from the encampment. And when the game was gone, the hungry hunters had no choice but to follow. It was pursue or perish.

And that was worst of all, the deepest of the pains: that when Sun had not favored the summer hunt, the winter camp held no rest for the Blackfeet. There could be no

111

pause in the ceaseless cycle of movement, no sending forth of roots, however shallow, into the Ground-Of-Many-Gifts.

It was to such a camp, heavy with the cries of children, the groans of old ones, and the howls of dogs, that the followers of The-Heavy-Runner had come in that winter of 1870.

A camp cursed by Sun.

Since the summer encampment there had been no rest for The-Heavy-Runner and his people. Without success they had tracked the northern herds beyond the Medicine Line, never staying more than a few sleeps in any place before folding their lodges and moving on, hoping always to find buffalo just beyond the next hill. But it had not been so, and at last the young men of the band, tired from the rigors of the hunt and from its disappointments, aroused by the encroachments of Napikwan and his riches, inflamed by drink, turned their energies from hunting buffalo to stealing horses.

Their defection doomed the hunt and all prospects for a winter camp of pleasure and content.

With the coming of Cold-Maker, the exhausted band, depleted and discouraged, drifted south out of the land of Northern-White-Men, across the line and into Montana, less for the purpose of hunting buffalo than in the dim, half-hearted hope that the Great Father might care for them and feed them at his house on the Teton. In that hope The-Heavy-Runner had met with Alfred Sully, only to find from the seizer chief he called friend that the Great Father had no food, no blankets for his Black-Footed-Children, that his only concern was for revenge on Owl-Child and the other young men who had murdered Four-Bears.

There on the first day of the new year, in the house of

the Great Father on the Teton, hope died within the breast of The-Heavy-Runner.

From the Great Father's house he led his ragged band to the Two-Medicine River, where a few renegade bulls and small, isolated groups of cows and calves had been sighted. They found none, however, and were forced to move on, driven by the certainty of starvation if they stopped, rarely staying in fixed camp more than a few days. As they moved, they were joined by the stragglers and starvelings of other bands, the old and infirm, the unwanted and unneeded, and by remnants of entire bands, reduced in numbers by desertions and deaths, too few or too weak to hunt, hopeful of finding support for life with The-Heavy-Runner and his followers. With them they brought nothing but their eroding hopes and dwindling will to live.

And the disease the Blackfeet knew as white-scabs. Smallpox.

By mid-January 1870, three or more of the four hundred followers of The-Heavy-Runner were dying each day, and each day more fell victim to the white-scabs. To the cries of children, the groans of old ones, and the howls of dogs, long the accustomed music of the stricken band, were now added the shrieks of the delirious dying and wails of the grieving survivors.

In such a state, the followers of The-Heavy-Runner came upon an abandoned camp site on the Big Bend of the Marias River, five miles below Medicine Creek, close beneath Black-Robe-Butte, and there, too weak to go on, they raised for the last time their lodges, painted and plain, their temples to the oneness of life and the glory of Sun.

Only a few days before, Raven-Quiver, Inspector General Hardie's trusted messenger Joseph Kipp, had visited the camp site, had seen there its previous occupants, and had identified them as the followers of Mountain-Chief, the Piegan band singled out by the white seizers for punishment. Shortly after the reconnoiter, however, Mountain-Chief had moved his camp sixteen miles down the Marias. But this was not known, not to Kipp nor to Philip Sheridan, not to Régis deTrobriand nor to Eugene Baker. And not to The-Heavy-Runner.

The-Heavy-Runner knew only that his people had by chance alone found a good place — if not to live, then at least to die — a place sheltered deep within the protecting walls of the Marias, with wood for their fires, and lodge sites made smooth by the recent occupants. There were even signs of buffalo nearby, and he quickly called the band's few warriors, those few who had remained and who were in good health, into council to organize a hunt.

On Saturday, January 22, 1870, in bitter cold and through deep, new-fallen snow, nearly every able-bodied man from the band of The-Heavy-Runner left the suffering camp on the Marias in search of meat.

The-Heavy-Runner spent the day within his lodge, smoking alone and in silence the pipe from his sacred bundle, again and again offering ritual smoke to Earth and Sun, to the four winds, and to his helper Raven, who sees all, seeking some sign, however slight, of guidance or of favor. Through the long hours of daylight there was none. But at day's end, the troubled warrior observed dark spots on the setting sun. The old chief's shoulders slumped in sadness. The sign was not good but bad, not a harbinger of hope but a clear warning of danger. Sun painted himself only for war.

During the night Cold-Maker raged over the Ground-Of-Many-Gifts. The-Heavy-Runner slept and dreamed of death.

114

*   *   *

Pale light had just begun to dilute the darkness of the eastern sky when the sounds, innocent explosions like the popping of autumn corn or the cracking of winter twigs, rattled through the lodge of The-Heavy-Runner, rousing him from his restless sleep. Inside the lodge, no light of dawn yet reached. Only embers of the fire, dimly pulsing and glowing, pierced the black, like mossy beds of brightness against a forest floor. What was this clatter reaching his ears? Trapped between night's shadows and day's dreams, without reality, thought, or belief, brain and body alike struggling for balance, The-Heavy-Runner walked to the entrance of his lodge, pushed aside the buffalo hide, and peered into the icy gloom of Sunday morning, January 23, 1870.

What he saw seemed in no way ominous.

From above the camp, strung tightly along the high bank of the Marias overlooking the lodges, tiny tongues of flame flared in the pre-dawn sky. Each ignited sharply, blazed warmly for an instant, a colorful patch in a scene without color, then faded, echoing away through the still, cold air with a crisp and cheerful crackling. The-Heavy-Runner stood watching and listening for a moment, without fear, fascinated by the bright torches and lively reports, as by a summer star shower or spring storm, far off in the unreachable recesses of the Backbone.

But as he woke, he wondered first and then knew.

Knew the eyes of death would glitter like these torches, knew death's breath would rattle like this popping corn, and be as cold.

He knew the sign from Sun had been true. Seizers had come in the frozen silence of night to surround his village and make war. The tongues of flame and echoing clatter

115

came from the mouths of their many-shot thundersticks.

The-Heavy-Runner heard the dogs howl and the people cry, and knew death stalked his children.

They have come in search of Owl-Child and the other murderers of Four-Bears, the old chief thought. They believe this to be the camp of the renegades. They believe me and my people to be enemies of the whites, and they wish to kill us.

He would tell them of their mistake.

From its elkskin pouch, he took the paper given him by Alfred Sully, the seizer chief, the paper which proved he was a man of peace, a friend and brother to the whites. He moved in haste, but with a quiet calm, for he knew the paper would save his people. Holding his bright blanket close about him with his left hand, the precious document held high over his head in his right, The-Heavy-Runner, cautious, gentle, aging chief of the Piegans, stepped from his lodge and approached the line of fire, walking slowly and solemnly, so as not to startle or provoke the seizers.

As he did so, the shooting stopped, the tongues of flame disappeared. No echoes of gunfire were heard. Only the voice of The-Heavy-Runner, resonant and strong.

I am The-Heavy-Runner, he called. I am friend to the whites. Do not shoot my people. We wish only peace with the whites. See! This paper from your chief says my words are true. My heart is with you. Do not shoot us.

My people are cold and hungry, he called. The white-scabs burn among us and we die. We have little food. Our young men have left camp to hunt. We are only the weak and the old left here, women and children, and the sick. Do not shoot us.

It is Owl-Child you seek, he called, holding his blanket tighter about him, shaking the paper above his head,

116

walking slowly, carefully away from his lodges, toward the Marias. You have made a mistake. Owl-Child is not here. The murderers of Four-Bears are not here. There are no enemies of the whites in this camp. Do not shoot us.

The-Heavy-Runner is your friend, he called. The-Heavy-Runner is your brother. The paper says my words are true.

As he spoke a single shot sounded. The old man slumped, staggered, but did not fall. His voice faltered but did not fail.

Do not shoot us, he called. We are friends. We are your brothers.

But the single shot had triggered others. Once more flickers and flares dotted the paling sky. Once more the frozen air crackled and popped.

And the old man fell.

For a moment, dark against the snow, he struggled to rise. But his eyes were already dim. His voice, straining reflexively to be heard, was soundless. His blood was cooling, his heart at rest.

The eyes that had seen something closed. Death had come for The-Heavy-Runner.

*   *   *

"I slept," spoke Black-Antelope, "and was wakened from sleep by the thunder of guns.

"I knew the seizers had come, because the guns were many-shots. I tried to wake Yellow-Weasel-Woman, but she was too weak from the white-scabs to move. I ran alone from my lodge, into the darkness.

"I saw The-Heavy-Runner come from his painted lodge. He had no weapon. He walked slowly, and looked very tall against the snow. Before him, raised high over his head, he carried the paper our Father had given him. He called out to the seizers as he walked. 'I am The-Heavy-Runner, friend to the whites. My people are good and peaceful people. Do not shoot us.'

"Many bullets flew, and he fell dead. I ran to the timber and lay watching and afraid.

"From the high banks of the river the seizers were shooting. The sounds of their many-shots filled my ears. From all around us, across the river, I heard the seizers shouting. Ah, so many of them. I knew we would that day join our departed ones in the Sand Hills.

"I saw the bullets tear our lodge covers, and from inside I heard the songs of death. The old ones moaned and sang their death songs. Our women screamed, and their screams joined the cries of the babies held close to their breasts. Oh, how the sounds burned my ears. To know how many would die, and we so weak, so sick and old we could not fight.

"My heart was full. My eyes rained. I prayed to Sun that our warriors might return and punish the seizers, but he did not hear me.

"Few left their lodges to shoot back at the seizers or to run. Those that ran were quickly dead, for the seizers were around me in the timber behind our camp, also. Those who tried to escape ran right into their guns. There was no escape. I lay very quiet, making no sound and no movement, and the seizers did not see me. I closed myself to the cold and did not feel the snow, and so my life was spared.

"For a long time the seizers from across the river shot into the camp. With the coming of day I could see the puffs of smoke from their guns as they fired, again and again, from low to the ground. And I watched as they went back to wagons for more bullets, then returned to their places and shot still again.

118

"When the sky became light and the seizers could see better, they aimed their guns at the bindings of our lodges, shooting them away until the lodge covers fell into our fires. Many that were not killed by the bullets were burned to death or smothered within their own lodges.

"Not until Sun stood straight in the sky did the seizers stop shooting. From before the coming of day to its middle, they had been shooting into the village. It seemed to me none could still be living.

"And yet I knew some must live, for although the many-shots now were silent, the screams of our women and children and the howlings of our hurt and frightened dogs filled the air. They were sounds to make water of stone. No man could hear such sounds and not mourn, for such are the sounds of the world's ending, when all must die.

"Their shooting done, the seizers ran into our camp like stampeding buffalo, to finish the work which they had begun. Each lodge which still stood they shot into with their guns and cut into with their knives until it fell. All the lodges but two they destroyed, and these two — one of them the painted lodge of The-Heavy-Runner — they left standing. To them they took any women and children who had lived through the shooting and the collapse of their lodges. These few they spared, and took them to the standing lodges.

"But any of our men who still lived they shot and killed as they left their lodges.

"I watched them tear down my lodge, in which Yellow-Weasel-Woman still was. My chest ached, for I did not know if she was alive or dead. I watched and watched for a sign that she lived, but there was none.

"The seizers laughed and joked as they moved from lodge to lodge, firing more shots into whatever moved or made a sound. They picked through whatever they found of value, clothing or weapons, and kept it for themselves. What was left they piled up beside the fallen lodges to burn. They piled what little food we still had, together with our winter robes and moccasins, all on top of the lodge covers and set fire to them. The dead were still inside, and some sick and some wounded. The seizers tried to burn everything.

"But it did not burn well.

"Late in the day the seizers turned loose the women and children they had kept in the two lodges still standing. There was much confusion and noise. Later the women told us the seizers had seen some with white-scabs and had turned all loose and told them to leave. The seizers were very afraid. The women and children were afraid also, and did not know where to go. They were hungry and had no food. They were sick and had no medicine. They were cold and had no robes. And in that condition the seizers turned them loose to go.

"Soon after that, the seizers left the camp, tearing down the last two lodges as they left, and taking with them all our horses.

"Those of us who lived, who had escaped to the trees in the early dark, came then from the timber to mourn. I sat before my fallen lodge, still smoking but not on fire, and could not lift the cover to look at Yellow-Weasel-Woman.

"She was a good old woman. She never hurt the whites. Why did they have to kill her?

"Now I was alone, and wished that I, too, were dead."

*　　*　　*

Before nightfall, three hunters from the camp of Mountain-Chief came upon the band of pitiful refugees, women and children and old ones, from the ravaged camp and returned-with them to it.

"They stared and stared at our fallen, half-burned lodges," recalled Bear-Head, "at our dead, lying here and there, and could hardly believe what they saw. They rode over to us, asked what had happened, and when we had told them of the white seizers' sudden attack upon us, it was long before they could speak. And then they said that we were to live with them; they would take care of us poor bereaved ones.

"That night the white seizers did not closely watch the hundreds of horses that they had taken from us. We managed to get back about half of the great herd and drive them down to Mountain-Chief's camp.

"During the day our buffalo hunters returned. With many horses loaded with meat and hides, they came singing, laughing, down into the valley, only to find their dear ones under their ruined lodges.

"As best we could we buried our dead — a terrible, grieving task it was — and counted them: fifteen men, ninety women, fifty children. Forty-four lodges and lodge furnishings destroyed, and hundreds of horses stolen.

"Haiya! Haiya!"

*   *   *

During the long night of Monday, January 24, 1870, in his sadness and his mercy, Cold-Maker cried for the people of the Ground-Of-Many-Gifts. His tears fell as a gentle snow, bandaging the wounded earth, burying her slaughtered children.

No sound was heard but his sobbing breath.

By morning no trace could be seen of The-Heavy-Runner or of his people who had lived in that place. They had vanished from Sun's sight.

"The expedition started on the morning of the 19th inst., under the command of Colonel Baker," read a January 23 report from Fort Shaw, published in the *Helena Daily Herald*. "We are patiently waiting to hear the result."

It was not long in coming.

"On Sunday morning the 23rd at daybreak, Col. Baker surprised the camp of Bear-Chief, a hostile Piegan — thirty lodges — on the Marias," deTrobriand cabled Hancock on January 26.

"The attack was a complete success, no more than four or five escaped. Three Bloods and one whiskey trader happening to be in the hostile camp are reported killed. Some wounded soldiers said to be with the train.

"The column was going on to strike the camp of Mountain-Chief when last heard of," he concluded.

Hancock replied the next day, expressing his hope that "Colonel Baker has been as successful...as seems to be indicated," and that "the pursuit of Mountain-Chief's band will terminate as successfully and creditably to all concerned."

"The expedition is a complete success," deTrobriand assured him on January 28.

"Colonel Baker just returned, having killed 173 Piegans, destroyed 44 lodges with all their winter supplies, robes, etc., and captured over 300 horses," he reported. "Most of the murderers and marauders of last summer are killed."

Unfortunately, he continued, Mountain-Chief and Owl-Child "escaped with a few of their followers."

The frontier press was unconcerned by their escape.

122

"Tidings arrived here this afternoon of our Indian hunters," announced the *Herald* on January 28. "It is reported that they fell in with 'Son-Of-Mountain-Chief's' band and had a fight the result being the annihilation of this most murderous company of red devils, and the killing or wounding of about twenty of our boys."

Perhaps not twenty. Regis deTrobriand scaled down the losses in his official dispatch.

"Colonel Baker lost one killed and one wounded," he told the *Herald*.

"Our loss — one man killed and one man accidentally wounded," cabled Philip Sheridan to General of the Army Sherman, on January 29, "by falling off his horse."

If Sheridan was disappointed by the escape of the two most wanted of the Piegan raiders, or questioned why friendly casualties in a major engagement had been so light, he did not mention it in his January 29 report to Sherman, and joined deTrobriand in terming the expedition a "complete success."

Hancock, too, was pleased, and cabled to deTrobriand his "warmest thanks for the handsome success obtained in the expedition against the Piegans."

"I only await the official details," he said, "to proclaim in orders my sense of the gallant and arduous service of the troops, and to do full justice to all concerned."

"Never was anything like it seen in Montana," wrote Regis deTrobriand to his daughter. "The settlers haven't raised a statue to me, but I am content that...I shall leave behind me this memory of my passage."

The frontier press was equally delighted.

"The deed is done," reported the *Daily Herald* on February 2, "the murder of Malcolm Clarke has been avenged; the guilty Indians have been punished, and a terrible warning has been given to others of our red-

123

skinned brethren, who may be inclined to live by murdering and plundering the white man."

The *Herald* continued with a candid account of the events of January 23 on the banks of the Marias River.

"The troops...surprised the camp of Bear-Chief," the paper reported. "The surprise was so perfect that the redskins fired but few shots. From all I can learn, the Indians were perfectly paralyzed with fright, and were mostly shot in their teepees. The women and children, so far as was practicable, were spared, but to the men no quarter was given. Mountain-Chief and a few others effected their escape. All the rest of the men were killed, and their camp...burned over their dead bodies.

"Probably there was not a soldier there who would not rather have seen a hard fight," the *Herald* commented, "but this was not to be.

"It was the last step; a terrible, but also a just and effective one."

Regis de Trobriand agreed.

"The Bloods, terrified by the punishment of the Piegans, deem it very fortunate not to have brought upon themselves such a severe retribution, and will carefully avoid giving offense to the white residents of the Territory," he reported to Hancock on February 2.

"As for the Piegans, they are completely cowed. They had never dreamed of such an execution, and the blow is more telling for being so entirely unexpected."

The citizens of the Montana town of Highland summed it up.

"Whereas, the U.S. soldiers under command of Colonel Baker, did...wipe out certain red fiends known as Piegan Indians," they resolved, therefore, "that we most heartily and sincerely indorse the manner of treaty then and there made with those and all others of our red

124

brethren who inhabit the soil of Montana."

"Considered in a military view the expedition was a complete and brilliant success," reported the *New North-West* on February 4.

"The Indians were the aggressors...they spared not age or sex, and so they have been slain. They repaid peace with powder, kindness with contempt, friendship with fire, and sustenance with theft. They compelled war and have perished."

The paper passed along an anecdote which reflected its feelings:

> "Will the Indians remain quiet now, do you think?" asked an anxious settler of Lieutenant Doane, of the Cavalry, when the expedition was returning from the Marias.
>
> "Well, I can't say," returned the Lieutenant, "but there are certainly one hundred and seventy-three very good arguments in favor of their remaining quiet, lying out on the Marias!"

Two discordant notes sounded louder with each passing day, however, disrupting the chorus of praise for Colonel Baker and his expedition.

The first concerned the early, unofficial count of casualties among the Piegans, a count which showed an unusually high number of women and children, one hundred or more. Anticipating the outrage of Eastern "philanthropists" when the character of the Indian casualties became known, newspapers sympathetic to the Army and its frontier mission undertook in advance to justify their deaths.

"The Indians are reported to have fought desperately," wrote the *Chicago Tribune* on February 3, "men, women, and children joining in the battle. It is feared some of the women and children were killed in the melee, but is hoped not many.

"In Indian attacks, where all fight," the *Tribune* continued, "the killing of a few women and children is always unavoidable. The officers do all in their power to prevent it, but they are unable to guide the bullets of their troopers."

If the age and sex of the dead Piegans provided the first disharmony, their names sounded the second.

In earlier communiqués, Regis deTrobriand and Inspector General Hardie had identified 15 warriors accused of criminal acts: Mountain-Chief, his two sons, Owl-Child, Eagle's-Rib, Bear-Chief, Black-Bear, Black-Weasel, Crow-Top, Star, Red-Horn, Under-Bull, Bull's Head, The-Cut-Hand, and White-Man's-Dog.

Of these, deTrobriand reported to Hancock on February 2, only Red-Horn was known to have been killed in the attack. Eagle's-Rib was reported seriously wounded. Bear-Chief, too, was believed to have been killed, although the report had not come from Baker. All others had either not been at the camp or had escaped unharmed.

And unfortunately, among the 173 Piegans who had been killed, he added, was The-Heavy-Runner.

"It is to be regretted that a friendly chief who had met Gen. Sully in council three weeks before should have perished by our bullets," he told Hancock, "but at the same time his death is not without some salutary teachings by showing to the friendly Indians what heavy risks they run in keeping intercourse with the hostile ones."

This matter must be investigated, and the facts obtained. It is shameful to have such statements published by authority, if they are false; it is terrible to think of what happened, if they are true.

New York Tribune
February 26, 1870

Major Eugene Baker, General Alfred Sully, General Philippe Regis deTrobriand

Victory or Massacre?
January 29 to March 29, 1870

LONG BEFORE Colonel Eugene M. Baker and his troops of the Second Cavalry and Thirteenth Infantry returned to Fort Shaw, rumors regarding their campaign on the Marias spread throughout Montana Territory. Far from winning a hotly-contested victory over hostile bands, went the reports, Baker had attacked a friendly and defenseless village.

From escaped Indians and white traders alike, the rumors reached Alfred Sully in Helena.

In a cable to Indian Commissioner Ely S. Parker on January 29, Sully described the first newspaper accounts of the engagement as "greatly exaggerated," and promised a "true report" as soon as the facts became known.

"I have received so many conflicting reports of this matter," he wrote the following day, "that I have delayed to make any report to you about it till I can sift the matter and make up my mind."

He was already convinced, however, that Baker had attacked the wrong band. He did not know if Baker had erred innocently or by intent, or whether Baker's men had committed the atrocities attributed to them, but whatever the case, he feared — as had Régis deTrobriand earlier — that the misdirected attack might well unite Piegans, Bloods, and Northern Blackfeet in war against the whites.

"I think difficulties with Indians in this Territory during the winter very probable," he wrote on January 30. "The late attack may possibly excite the nation to open war."

As for the truth of the other charges against Colonel Baker and his men, Sully decided to first communicate his concern to deTrobriand.

"I have seen reports of Colonel Baker's attack on the Indians where it states that one hundred and seventy-three were killed," he cabled on February 1. "How many of these killed were men? It has been reported to me that there were only twenty or thirty, the rest women and children. These reports come from citizens, half-breeds, and Indians."

Determined to silence the rumors before Sully's support gave them broader circulation and additional credence, deTrobriand responded immediately.

"As to what you say in regard to the operations of Colonel Baker against the Piegans," he wrote Sully on February 3, "I should be sorry to think that you put any faith in the idle rumors and false reports spread by some whiskey smugglers from Benton, whose poisonous drug was found in plenty in the Indian camps, and by other croakers to whom the peace of the Territory and the security of its residents are of little or no weight, compared with their private interests in trade.

"To specify," deTrobriand went on, "it is currently reported that you stated as fact the very thing you mention in your letter as the report of half-breeds and Indians; and, to be more explicit, you are alleged to have said that we had killed only the old women and children; that the warriors were all away hunting, and that when they heard from their camp they sent word to Colonel Baker that they were coming to fight him if he would wait for them, and that Colonel Baker, hearing the news, hastened away back to Fort Shaw.

"This I would not mention if it were not to show you what reports of all sorts are in circulation," he added, "and how unwise it would be to give them any credence, unless ascertained by positive information."

On February 6, Lieutenant William B. Pease, Sully's agent to the Blackfeet, forwarded the "positive information" he had received with respect to casualties among the followers of The-Heavy-Runner.

"Of the one hundred and seventy-three killed on the 23rd," he wrote Sully, "thirty-three were men. Of them, fifteen only were such as are called by them as young or fighting men. Ninety were women. The remaining fifty were children, none older than twelve years and many of them in their mother's arms."

Pease also confirmed that the camp had been "suffering severely with smallpox," adding that the surviving Blackfeet "express themselves as being much frightened, and not disposed to retaliate upon the whites for the death of their friends." Still, the agent said, "it is hardly reasonable to expect that they will be satisfied without the revenge that an Indian's nature craves."

Four days later, Sully forwarded the report of his agent (the result of two meetings with surviving Piegan chiefs) to Washington, cautioning that it was "entirely what the Indians say of the affair, and of course it is natural to suppose it is prejudiced in their own favor."

It was to be regretted, he said, "that Mountain-Chief's was not the band that suffered...but they, though most guilty, escaped and got across the line.

"I refrain from making any comment on the reported

unnecessary and uncalled-for cruelty on the part of the soldiers," he concluded. "Both sides should be heard before one can justly make up his mind on the matter."

They soon would be.

*   *   *

"At last," wrote Vincent Collyer, secretary to the Board of Indian Commissioners, on February 22, "the sickening details of Colonel Baker's attack...have been received."

In a letter to his fellow Commissioners, watchdogs of the nation's Indian policies and programs, Collyer revealed the casualty figures and other incidents reported by Lt. Pease, and opened to public debate the issue of the Army's conduct in the punishment of the Piegans.

Collyer's comments shocked the liberal Eastern press, which, on February 23, gave prominent coverage to his letter regarding the Piegans; and the United States Congress, which, two days later, heard the letter read into the record of proceedings of the House of Representatives.

Congressman Aaron Sargent of California called Baker's campaign an "act of cruelty...at which our children will blush.

"I say there is no warrant in the laws of God or of man for destroying women and children merely because their husbands and fathers may be marauders.

"I say that civilization shudders at horrors like this," Sargent said, and most of his colleagues agreed.

"I shall wash my hands of all responsibility for this system of warfare," thundered Congressman Daniel Voorhees of Indiana. "It cannot be justified here or before the country; it cannot be justified before the civilization of the age, or in the sight of God or man."

Added Congressman Charles Eldridge of Wisconsin: "If

132

they are the wards of the Government, then we who are taking care of them are the most barbarous people on earth. We are the worst guardians ever heard of in thus sacrificing the wards intrusted to our care."

Even Congressman Halbert Paine of Wisconsin, usually an unquestioning supporter of the Army and its actions, could only express the hope that a mistake had been made, and that Collyer's report referred to some expedition other than that ordered by General Sheridan against the Piegans.

"I should be very unwilling to leave resting upon General Sheridan...the stigma which would naturally attach by reason of the report of Mr. Collyer, if unexplained," Paine told his colleagues. "Certainly if he is responsible for that massacre of women and children the responsibility is a very grave one."

Only Congressman Job Stevenson of Ohio initially defended the orders and actions of the military in the Piegan expedition, at the same time setting the stage for the more detailed defense which would follow in the days ahead.

"I rise," he said, "...to enter my protest against these sweeping condemnations of the Government and its officers. I for one, if I stand alone, avow my approval of the sentiment expressed in the orders of General Sheridan. They express the sentiments of war, and I have always believed...that in war the most vigorous policy is not only the best policy, but is the most merciful policy. General Sheridan says we must strike a blow with telling effect, and that is the only way to make war."

As for the slaughter of women and children, said Stevenson, it is unavoidable, perhaps even desirable. "These savages who themselves never care for age or sex, these savages whose women and children make war on white women and children, these savages who dance for joy around the burning stake, these savages whose women and children are instruments and demons of torture to white women and children, are only to be warred upon, when you war at all, by a war of extermination," he told the House.

But Stevenson was dismissed by his colleagues as "bellicose" and "bloodthirsty." "I should be amazed, if anything could amaze me," commented Congressman Voorhees, "that any gentlemen could be found here to enter even a partial plea for such a monstrous transaction."

Lt. Gen. Philip H. Sheridan and Col. Eugene M. Baker had few friends on the floor of the House of Representatives on Friday, February 25, 1870.

And fewer still in the nation's newspapers as they reported the controversy.

"These are dreadful statements," editorialized the New York *Tribune* on February 26, "which Mr. Paine declared in the House he could not believe; but he said that Gen. Sheridan's responsibility was certainly very grave if he had ordered the massacre.

"This matter must be investigated," the newspaper continued, "and the facts obtained. It is shameful to have such statements published by authority, if they are false; it is terrible to think of what happened, if they are true."

But if the *Tribune* of New York was doubtful, the *Tribune* of Chicago was not.

"The account given by Vincent Collyer did not by any means present the worst features of the affair," commented the newspaper on March 3. "There is nothing in the records of the Indian Office which surpasses the atrocities detailed in this paper. Several members of the House have been informed of its character, and steps are pretty sure to be taken in Congress looking to dismissing from the service those officers directly responsible for the atrocities committed."

Two days later, on March 5, the *Chicago Tribune* further reported that General Sully had written to the Indian Bureau "expressing grave doubt whether the band surprised and murdered had taken any part in the late depredations," and adding new figures from Lt. Pease to the effect that "the lives of eighteen women and nineteen children, none of them more than three years of age, and many of them much younger, some of whom were wounded, were not spared by the soldiers."

Wrote the paper: "The affair is looked on at the Interior Department as the most disgraceful butchery in the annals of our dealings with the Indians."

*   *   *

Farther west, the press disagreed with the *Tribune's* characterization of the campaign.

Publishing pertinent orders and reports from and between Generals Sheridan, Hancock, Hardie, and deTrobriand, Montana's *New North-West* on February 25 explained that it considered the documents "important as showing the authority the Montana officers had for the big strike," particularly "in view of the efforts that will probably be made to guillotine the superior officers engaged in the Marias expedition" — efforts the *New North-West* deplored.

For all that, however, the paper was not optimistic that the reports would settle matters, warning its readers that "...all the namby-pamby, sniffling old maid sentimentalists of both sexes who leave most of their brains on their handkerchiefs when under excitement, will join the jargon of discontent."

And when the House of Representatives reconvened on

Monday, February 28, after the weekend recess, the initial tone of the debate justified the *New North-West's* warnings.

Damning the "system of indiscriminate slaughter that knows neither age nor sex," Congressman Samuel Axtell of California branded it "a barbarous policy, that cannot be too much reprehended by all good men; all men who love humanity because it is humanity, love men and women because they are men and women, ought to frown it down."

Congressmen from across the nation, from Fernando Wood of New York to Aaron Sargent of California, condemned the campaign against the Piegans, expressing their shock at Sheridan's plan and their outrage at Baker's execution of it. "I am amazed," repeated Congressman Voorhees, "that gentlemen on this floor can be found to rise in the face of the American people and advocate that our policy of warfare upon the Indians shall partake of the character of the massacre of the Piegan Indians."

But on the last day of February 1870, the House held many such gentlemen. Caught unprepared at the earlier session, they were now determined to turn the tide of protest which threatened not just the careers of Sheridan, deTrobriand, and Baker, but the Army's influence in government, its standing on the frontier, and its military strategy for controlling the Indians.

Not surprisingly, Congressman James T. Cavanaugh of Montana led the counterattack.

While acknowledging the apparent harshness of a winter campaign, he argued that no other season offered reasonable prospect of success for chastising a people he accused of "atrocities that shock humanity — atrocities that are nameless... nameless mutilations of both men and women...witnessed by my own eyes."

136

"It is in the summer that they come down upon our houses, our villages, our towns, and slaughter our people," he explained, and "the only place where you can strike the Indian is to strike him in his lodge and in his camp in mid-winter."

Repeating his stand on the issue of casualties among what appeared to be non-combatants, Ohio's Congressman Stevenson emphasized that it was an unfortunate but unavoidable result of Indian-style warfare.

"If women will fight with guns in their hands, if children be put upon the ramparts with guns in their hands, they may be killed," he said.

But the killing of women and children and the necessity of mid-winter military strikes against Indian camps were side issues only. At the heart of the debate lay the continuing question of whether advocates of war or of peace with the Indians would prevail. It was left to Congressman Richard McCormick of Arizona to address that fundamental issue.

He did so forthrightly.

"I propose a vigorous war party against Indians who are known to be hostile," McCormick said.

"If war is necessary, absolutely necessary, with any of the Indians — and I believe it is — let us have war in every sense of the term; let us strike heavy and strike hard.

"This is the humane way; this is the economical way; this is the only way."

Montana's Congressman Cavanaugh enthusiastically echoed McCormick's sentiments.

"I endorse the order of General Phil Sheridan," he told the House. "I endorse the act of General Hancock. I endorse the conduct of Colonel Baker."

"I desire to ask the gentleman," interrupted Congressman George Hoar of Massachusetts, "if he means to say that he approves the killing of these women and children in cold blood, when there were no arms in their hands."

"I will answer the question fairly and squarely," replied Cavanaugh, "in the words of General Harney after the battle of Ash Hollow, years ago...they are nits, and will become lice. I endorse...the act of Colonel Baker."

Encouraged by stiffening resistance within Congress to the attacks on Sheridan and Baker, the *New North-West* grew more hopeful than it had been a week earlier.

"The strife for the head of Baker has begun in Congress," it wrote on March 4. "They sigh and yearn much and will not be comforted until the head of Baker is presented on a charger, or he is flayed alive."

But, continued the paper, they would sigh in vain. "This Indian Ring," it predicted, "is in its last throes.

"The Ring failed in its efforts for a head after Washita because Sheridan stood by his faithful subordinates. We have not less confidence in his manliness now, and the vindication of Baker."

Their confidence, as events would prove, was well placed.

*   *   *

However favorable the long-term prospects for Colonel Baker's vindication, the short term held serious concerns for General of The Army William Tecumseh Sherman, among the most pressing of which was the fact that an official Army report of Baker's expedition had yet to be submitted.

As early as January 29 he had requested the prompt preparation of a report by Baker. By February 26, he was desperate. Embarrassing questions were being asked in

138

Congress, and he had no answers.

"Have you collected all the reports in regard to Colonel Baker's fight with the Piegans?" he asked Sheridan. "If so, please forward at once."

What he received in reply was not Baker's official report. More than a month after the campaign, Sheridan still had no such report to submit.

"Colonel Baker could not make out his report at Fort Shaw," he explained on February 28, "as he was obliged to return immediately to Fort Ellis to get shelter for his horses and men."

But Sheridan did have other matters to report.

"I see that Mr. Vincent Collyer is out again in a sensational letter," he wrote. "Why did he not mention that Colonel Baker had captured over one hundred women and children? This he suppressed in order to do injustice to that officer by deceiving the kind-hearted public."

To correct the misimpression, Sheridan continued with a background report on Indian atrocities.

"Since 1862," he told Sherman, "at least eight hundred men, women and children have been murdered within the limits of my present command, in most fiendish manner, the men usually scalped and mutilated, their privates cut off and placed in their mouths; women ravished sometimes fifty and sixty times in succession, then killed and scalped, sticks stuck up their persons before and after death. I have myself conversed with one woman, who, while some months gone in pregnancy, was ravished over thirty times successively by different Indians, becoming insensible two or three times during this fearful ordeal; and each time on recovering consciousness, mutely appealing for mercy, if not for herself, for her unborn child. Also another woman ravished with more fearful brutality, over forty times, and the last sticking the point of his saber up the person of the woman. I could give the names of these women," he added, "were it not for delicacy."

"It would appear," Sheridan concluded, "that Mr. Vincent Collyer wants this work to go on."

Collyer replied without delay, noting on March 3 that "Gen. Sheridan strikes out at me almost as wildly as he did at the poor Piegans, and with about as much justice." Continued Collyer in his letter to the Board of Indian Commissioners: "If the General thinks that it relieves the blackness of the picture any to say that in addition to the 90 women and 50 children, sick with the smallpox, killed, there were 100 women and children also taken prisoners, I will add it now.

"Lieut. Pease...does not make it so bad as that," Collyer added. "He says there were 18 women and 19 children (none over three years, and the majority much younger), some of whom were wounded, taken prisoners."

Nor did Collyer confine his rebuke of Sheridan to the question of prisoners taken.

"Of the outrages against the poor settlers of the border," he wrote, "he says that I 'want it to go on.' No, General, you know you are not justified in any such inference as this. Because I pull aside the curtain and let the American people see what you call a 'great victory over the Indians,' it does not follow that we do not want the *men* who performed the horrid crimes with so much zest justly punished."

Sherman acknowledged the report less critically.

"Don't be unhappy about Indian affairs," he cabled Sheridan on March 5.

"There are two classes of people, one demanding utter extinction of the Indians, and the other full of love for their conversion to civilization and Christianity. Unfortunately, the Army stands between and gets cuffs from both sides."

140

For all that, however, the General of the Army still needed the official account, and needed it badly. "Let us have Baker's full report," he urged once more, "as soon as possible."

Two days later, an additional line of defense occurred to Sherman.

"The Piegans were attacked on the application of General Sully and the Interior Department," he wrote Sheridan on March 7, "and that these should now be shocked at the result of their requisitions and endeavor to cast blame on you and Colonel Baker, is unfair.

"General Sully, by communicating by telegraph for the use of Mr. Collyer," he continued, "did an unsoldierlike and wrong act, and this will, in the end, stand to his discredit."

To the toll of the campaign on the Marias River could now be added whatever career prospects remained to General Alfred Sully.

*   *   *

Not until March 8, forty-five days after the attack, did General Sherman receive the official Army version of the events of January 23 at the Big Bend of the Marias River. Although dated February 18, Colonel Baker's report had been unaccountably delayed.

Why or by whom is not known.

Baker returned to Fort Shaw from the Marias River on Saturday, January 29, and to Fort Ellis from Fort Shaw on Sunday, February 6. Generals Sherman, Sheridan, and Hancock all urgently requested a prompt accounting. Resisting the pressure, he took nearly two weeks to submit the report. For being so long in preparation, it was remarkably brief.

After a concise chronicling of the march to the Marias, Baker reported that the "camp of Bear-Chief and Big-Horn" had been surprised at about eight o'clock on the morning of the 23rd. "We killed one hundred and seventy-three Indians," he said, "captured over one hundred women and children, and over three hundred horses.

"I ordered Lt. Doane to remain in this camp and destroy all the property," he explained, "while I marched down the river after the camp of Mountain-Chief. After marching sixteen miles, I found a camp of seven lodges that had been abandoned in great haste, leaving everything. The Indians had scattered in every direction, so that it was impossible to pursue them."

Adding that the women and children had been freed, "as it was ascertained that some of them had the small-pox," Baker concluded: "Too much credit cannot be given to the officers and men of the command for their conduct during the whole expedition."

"To this report I have but little to add," cabled deTrobriand in his letter of transmittal, dated the same day as Baker's account, February 18, but undelivered until March 4.

"It is most gratifying that my previsions were fully realized," he wrote, "and complete success was attained.

"This most desirable result has been accomplished chiefly by the activity, energy, and judgment with which Colonel Baker conducted the operations," he pointed out, "conforming himself in every respect to his instructions, and making the most of what was left to his discretion.

"I would therefore recommend that experienced and able officer to the approving commendation of superior headquarters, for a promotion by brevet as a just acknowledgment of his excellent conduct in this circumstance."

142

Hancock received Baker's report and deTrobriand's letter of transmittal on March 4, and he, too, had nothing of substance to add.

"Respectfully forwarded," he cabled Sheridan.

"As it was not known when Col. Baker's expedition received its orders that smallpox was in the camps, he was directed to attack, and it was supposed that the warriors belonging to those camps were all present. If they were not, as has since been alleged, it is presumed the fact was not known to Col. Baker until the attack ended."

Sheridan forwarded the correspondence to Sherman on March 8, along with the report of Inspector General Hardie, who, said Sheridan, "was sent especially to Montana, so that I might be fully satisfied of the guilt of the Indians."

To those accounts of the circumstances surrounding Baker's expedition against the Piegans the Army would add nothing more.

*   *   *

On March 12, 1870, a year after his confident claim that "The Indian wars are over," General Philip Sheridan issued General Order #1 officially commending Baker and his men for the "complete success" of their mission.

"The Lieutenant General cannot commend too highly the spirit and conduct of the troops and their commander," the Order read, "and...congratulates the citizens of Montana upon the reasonable prospect of future security for their property and lives."

The citizens of Montana accepted the congratulations with delight.

From Helena, General deTrobriand wrote his daughter of a "grand reception" held in honor of his role in the campaign.

"About half past six," he related, "the maitre d'hôtel, without saying anything, opened the window giving on the street, and immediately there commenced a serenade in my honor beneath torches.

"The crowd called me to the balcony. There I was on stage, my entrance applauded, acclaimed and introduced to the citizens by the favorite orator of the place. I astonished the natives by an improvised talk which was interrupted twenty times by applause, and when my peroration ended, three hurrahs and a 'tiger' for General Trobriand, Trobian, Troben, Trobridge, Trobin, and all the other indescribable names."

The Frenchman with the unpronounceable name had grown much in the esteem of the citizens of Montana.

The Eastern press, however, received the explanation of Colonel Baker and the proclamation of General Sheridan with continued skepticism.

"They do not deny the wholesale slaughter of Indian women and children," noted the New York *Tribune*.

"We may take that, therefore, as admitted."

Official Army accounts "designed to justify the cruel outrage," wrote the *Tribune* on March 12, "...merely serve to shift the responsibility from shoulder to shoulder, and fail utterly to show that the original reports of the violence and inhumanity of the troops were false or exaggerated. On the contrary, they more than confirm the first painful stories, and afford additional reasons for demanding that the responsibility shall be fixed and the offender punished."

As for Sheridan's General Order #1, said the paper, "It would have been in better taste if the congratulatory order now published had been withheld pending the official investigation."

144

It was not the opinions of the *Tribune,* however, that concerned Philip Sheridan, but the position of General Sherman, who made it clear he was not yet ready to accept Baker's report of February 18 as the final word on the matter.

"He does not report in detail as is proper and usual, the sex and kind of Indians actually left dead at the camp on the Marias," wrote Sherman, forwarding the report and accompanying documents to the Secretary of War on March 12.

"I will instruct General Sheridan to call on Colonel Baker for a fuller report on this point, to meet the public charge that of the number killed the greater were squaws and children."

On the same day he did.

"In view of the severe strictures in Congress on this act as one of horrible cruelty to women and children," he cabled General Sheridan, "I wish you would require, by telegraph, Colonel Baker to report especially on this point."

Replying on March 18, Sheridan once more began by cataloging the "fiendish" outrages committed by Indians — "the men scalped, the women ravished, and the brains of children bashed out."

"I have no hesitation in making my choice," Sheridan cabled. "I am going to stand by the people over whom I am placed and give them what protection I can."

But then he added a new argument.

"If a village is attacked," he explained, "and women and children killed, the responsibility is not with the soldier, but with the people whose crimes necessitate the attack.

"During the war, did any one hesitate to attack a village or town occupied by the enemy because women or children were within its limits? Did we cease to throw shells into Vicksburg or Atlanta because women or children were there?" he asked Sherman.

It was a defense new only to Baker's campaign against the Piegans. William Tecumseh Sherman had heard it before.

He had been the commander at the Civil War sieges of Vicksburg and Atlanta. He, like Baker, had been accused of taking the lives of innocent women and children. And in his defense, he, as Sheridan well knew, had used the argument that the instigators of war call upon themselves, by their crimes, retaliation without restraint.

"Those who struck the first blow and made war inevitable," Sherman said then, "ought not in fairness to reproach us for natural consequences." And: "This is cruel warfare, but the enemy has brought it upon himself by his own conduct."

"War is cruelty," he had concluded. "There is no use trying to reform it. The crueler it is, the sooner it will be over."

Sherman had maintained that his sieges of Vicksburg and Atlanta had conformed with the rules of war then in force, which read: "Commanders whenever admissable inform the enemy of their intention to bombard a place, so that the non-combatants and especially the women and children may be removed before the bombardment commences. But, it is no infraction of the common law of war to omit to inform the enemy. Surprise may be a necessity."

Now Sheridan maintained that Baker's attack on the Piegan camp conformed likewise to the articles of war. Surprise, he insisted, had been a necessity. The deaths of women and children, while regrettable, were unavoidable and no violation of the articles.

Baker's case, Sheridan now made clear, was Sherman's own, as was his defense. For Sherman to question Baker's

146

cause would be to prejudice his own.

While Sherman pondered this new twist of the case, the Eastern press remained unmoved. "Gen. Sheridan's special pleading in justification of the massacre of the Piegans," wrote the New York *Tribune* on March 24, "is not convincing.

"The attack on the Indian camp is not to be justified by the comparisons he quotes of the bombardment of Vicksburg and Atlanta. Both cities were fortified towns, garrisoned by great armies, and the bombardment of neither was begun until formal notice for the removal of women and children required by the rules of civilized war had been given. This usage was not practicable in the case of the Piegan camp, it is true; but that does not justify the acts perpetrated after the capture. There is nothing in what Gen. Sheridan says which should put a stop to any inquiry as to who is responsible for the outrage."

Sheridan knew the issue would not be decided by expressions of public support or opposition, however, but by the War Department's formal approval or censure of Baker and his conduct. With that knowledge, he now took up the suggestion made by Regis deTrobriand in his letter of February 18 forwarding Baker's initial report, and demanded that the Department promote Colonel Baker "as a just acknowledgment of his excellent conduct in this circumstance" and as a symbol of its endorsement of Sheridan's Indian-fighting philosophy for the plains.

Should his demand go unmet, he asked to be transferred from the plains command.

As always, Eastern and Western newspapers held differing views of Sheridan's demands and of their prospects.

Reported the New York *Tribune* on March 22: "President Grant has not sent Baker's name to the Senate for promotion, nor is there any chance of his doing so, nor would the Senate grant the promotion if his name were sent in. There is little doubt, however, that Gen. Sheridan's request for a new field of duty will be conceded."

Countered the *New North-West* of March 25: "It is thought the Department is favorably disposed to Gen. Sheridan, and will testify its approval of his course by recommending Colonel Baker for an additional brevet. This the General considers would be a sufficient indorsement of his policy, and would remove all cause for anxiety."

Time alone would prove the matter. In the meantime, Colonel Eugene Baker's campaign against the Piegans had become Philip Sheridan's personal cause and concern.

And for the present, its outcome remained in doubt.

*   *   *

In a military career spanning thirty years, Philip Sheridan had won a reputation as the Army's most thorough gatherer of field intelligence. He always knew the enemy's position, its strengths and weaknesses — and his own. He always had all the facts. It was in keeping with that reputation that he had ordered Inspector General Hardie to Montana in January, to evaluate the Indian situation there, and to advise him how to proceed against the Piegans. It was, finally, on Hardie's recommendation that he had approved Baker's strike against Mountain-Chief.

But now, with Baker's campaign under protest and his own career in jeopardy, Sheridan had betrayed his reputation. He had no facts.

Having staked that reputation in support of Baker, he still had no certain knowledge of what actually had taken

148

place at the Big Bend of the Marias River on the morning of January 23, 1870. He had the report of Lieutenant Pease, which called the campaign a massacre and accused Baker's men of atrocities; and he had the report of Colonel Baker, which said the battle had been fairly fought and won.

Sheridan did not know which version was true.

Had he known the truth, there would have been no necessity to call once again on Hardie.

"State to me by telegraph if the band of Piegans struck by Baker was guilty," he had Hardie cable deTrobriand on March 16. "How do you know of their guilt? How do you presume Baker knew state, age, sex and condition of people killed? Send for young Clarke. Get his affidavit. I want also Joseph Kipp's affidavit. Send them by mail."

The questions deTrobriand answered easily.

"The band of Piegans struck by Baker was guilty," he cabled in reply. "Lots of murderers and thieves among them. They boasted of it themselves, and announced that in early spring they would be down on the settlements, murdering and plundering.

"Baker never knew the state, age, sex, or condition of the Indians killed," he continued. "How could he? Quarter was given to all known in time as women and children."

The remainder of Hardie's inquiry, his requests for affidavits from Horace Clake and Joseph Kipp, two men "who had good reasons to see the Indians punished," would be more difficult.

"Now it remains for me to attend to that part of your message to be answered by mail," deTrobriand wrote on March 20.

"This part I do not very clearly understand.

"You request me to send for young Clarke and get his affidavit, and you mention that you also want Joe Kipp's

149

affidavit," deTrobriand went on, "but you don't say about what."

What information could Hardie want from Horace Clarke?

"Is it about the murder of Mr. Clarke by the Indians," he asked, "and about Horace Clarke being treacherously shot himself by Mountain-Chief's son? Or is it about the papers of the father found on the bodies of some of the Piegans killed by our men on the Marias?"

And to what could Hardie want Raven-Quiver to testify?

"Is it to the extent of the falsehood of Lieut. Pease in his report and to the real number of women and children killed?"

On that subject, deTrobriand continued, "I can tell you that...the total number is about 220 — out of which 70 were warriors or fighting men." Explaining the number of casualties among women, he added, was the fact that "a number were actually murdered by their husbands in order to save them (as they imagined) from the tortures among white men which are inflicted upon white women when captured by those red fiends."

Repeating his inability to decipher Hardie's further intent in requesting affidavits from Clarke and Kipp, deTrobriand pledged to "prepare and send to you any documents you may want, as soon as you let me know more explicitly than by your last telegram."

Regis deTrobriand, in fact, had the statements of Clarke and Kipp, and hoped his message was clear: They had nothing to say that Sheridan wanted to hear.

Horace Clarke's Statement

"I was in the Baker fight and personally knew The-Heavy-Runner, a good Indian and friend of the white people. His camp was practically wiped out. It is an undeniable fact that Col. Baker was drunk and did not know what he was doing. The hostile camp was Mountain-Chief's, and it was the camp we intended to strike. But owing to much excitement and confusion and misinformation, The-Heavy-Runner's camp was the sufferer and the victim of circumstances."

Joseph Kipp's Statement

"When the soldiers reached the camp of The-Heavy-Runner, this chief went toward them to tell them who he was and to explain his mission there, but the soldiers opened fire, and I myself counted 217 dead bodies after the firing had ceased. The-Heavy-Runner was shot and killed during this firing. All of the able-bodied Indians were out hunting, and those who were killed were the Chief and such Indians as could not hunt, being old men and women and children. The Indians did not return the fire of the soldiers. Only one shot was fired by any of the Indians, and this was after the general firing had ceased, when the soldiers rode through the camp and shot everything and every person that was alive if he saw that they had been injured. This soldier opened the flap of one of the tents, and after shooting inside started to ride away, when an Indian inside the tent drew his gun on this soldier and shot him in the neck or back of the head and knocked him from his horse. After the firing was over, the soldiers gathered up the bedding, clothing, and subsistence and piled them up with a lot of wood and burned everything."

151

General deTrobriand was certain he would hear no more from Hardie on the subject of the Piegan campaign. Sheridan was too deeply committed to the defense of Baker to persist in the pursuit of evidence unfavorable to the accused officer and the Army. As for his personal involvement in Baker's conduct, he wrote his daughter on March 18, "In my correspondence, my dispositions, and my instructions to Colonel Baker, there is not one word to form a basis for criticism.

"Sustained by the testimonials which I received in Helena on this matter, my attitude remains serenely amused and unmoved."

Trop Brillant Pour Etre Terni!

*   *   *

Only one major obstacle remained to be overcome, and on March 24 it was.

In a letter to Sheridan, released at the same time to the press, General of the Army Sherman restated in his own words and as his own opinion Sheridan's position regarding Baker's campaign — that it had been hard fought and fairly won.

"It is, of course," he wrote, "to be deplored that some of our people prefer to believe the story of the Piegan massacre as trumped up by interested parties at Benton, more than a hundred miles off, rather than the official report of Colonel Baker, who was on the spot, and is the responsible party."

For his own part, Sherman went on, "I prefer to believe that the majority of those killed at Mountain-Chief's camp were warriors; that the firing ceased the moment resistance was at an end; that quarter was given to all who asked for it: and that a hundred women and children were allowed to go free to join the other bands of the same tribe known to be camped nearby, rather than the absurd report that there were only thirteen warriors killed, and that all the balance were women and children, more or less afflicted with smallpox."

As for who had responsibility for military action having been taken at all, Sherman continued, "the Bureau officers had officially notified you of their inability to restrain these very Piegans, and had called on you to punish them for their repeated and increasing robberies and murders, and you had, as early as last October, laid down the plan for a winter surprise and attack, which plan was immediately sent to the Indian Bureau, eliciting no remonstrance.

"There is," he wrote, "no question at all of responsibility, save and except only as to whether Colonel Baker wantonly and cruelly killed women and children unresistingly, and this I never believed."

This brought him to the main point.

"We must," concluded the General of the Army, "sustain the officers on the spot who fulfill their orders."

*   *   *

The New York *Tribune* was as unimpressed as Sheridan was relieved with Sherman's stand.

"Inasmuch as he writes frankly and vigorously," commented the *Tribune* on March 25, "we are not sorry that Gen. Sherman seizes every opportunity to write and publish letters.

"But it would be better for his reputation if he indulged more in fact and less in pathos," the paper continued. "He

153

defends Col. Baker, but what he says affects but little the real issue; it does not lessen the responsibility for that outrage, nor render unnecessary the inquiry which ought to be made."

"We are glad to see that Gen. Sherman is able to entertain some doubts about the killing of women and children," the *Tribune* editorialized the following day. "We wish he would furnish some ground for disbelieving the statements published on this point."

Failing such evidence, said the paper, "the affair should be thoroughly investigated by the military authorities, under the direction of the Congress."

Agreement came from an unexpected source: Colonel Eugene M. Baker.

"All the officers of the command ask at the hands of the authorities," he wrote General Sheridan on March 23, "is a full and complete investigation of the campaign, and less than this cannot, in justice, be conceded to them."

Baker selected his follow-up report, the "fuller" report solicited by General Sherman on March 12 "to meet the public charge that of the number killed the greater part were squaws and children," as the vehicle for his request.

But first he reported the casualty figures Sherman had sent for.

"After having made *every* effort to get the judgment of the officers of the command," Baker wrote, "I am satisfied that the following numbers approximate as nearly to the exact truth as any estimate can possibly be made — that the number killed was one hundred and seventy-three. Of those there were one hundred and twenty able men, fifty-three women and children; that of captives (afterward released), there were of women and children one hundred and forty.

"I believe," he continued, "that every effort was made

by officers and men to save the non-combatants, and that such women and children as were killed were killed accidentally."

Of one thing Baker was certain.

"The reports published in the eastern newspapers, purporting to come from General Alfred Sully, are wholly and maliciously false," he told Sheridan, "and if he has authorized them he knew them to be false; if he has given authority to these slanders, I can only suppose it is that attention may be drawn away from the manifest irregularities and inefficiency that mark the conduct of Indian affairs under his direction in this Territory.

"It seems incredible," he went on, "that the false assertions of two officers, General Sully and Lieutenant Pease, neither of whom have made any effort to inform themselves in the matter, should outweigh the reports of those who were engaged in the fight, and feel that they have nothing to palliate or concede in their conduct."

Concluding with his call for a "full and complete investigation" of the campaign, Colonel Eugene M. Baker was not again heard from officially on the expedition, which came to bear his name: the Baker Massacre.

It was, in the opinion of the New York *Tribune,* an unconvincing note on which to conclude his participation.

Wrote the paper on March 29: "Col. Baker adds his testimony to that of Generals Sheridan and Sherman in the effort to show that there was nothing inhuman in the Piegan massacre. But there is a suspicious look about the figures.

"The story becomes more painful and the act less justifiable with each explanation."

Sherman forwarded Baker's report to the Secretary of War on March 28, noting that "the officers engaged in that expedition desire a thorough investigation."

Such an investigation could be conducted, he added, "if you deem the good of the serice requires it."

In a letter to General Sheridan written the same day, Sherman asked him to tell Baker that "we will give him the benefit of an official investigation" under one condition: "If any responsible parties will father the reports that have been so extensively published."

None came forward.

"You may assure Colonel Baker," wrote Sherman to Sheridan, "that no amount of clamor has shaken our confidence in him and his officers."

*   *   *

So did the Army close the official record of Colonel Eugene M. Baker's expedition against the Blackfeet.

And with that act, the national balance had in fact been restored.

The Eastern establishment had given tongue to its outrage; the frontier had reaffirmed its right to exterminate Indians. Baker finally lost his promotion; Sheridan continued in command of Indian country.

Content, the nation turned its attention to the impending visit of the Sioux war chiefs, Red Cloud and Spotted Tail, to Washington, and put behind it the unfortunate incident on the Marias.

Father, pity us. Discover now to us all your will. Cover the blood that was shed on the earth. Do not hate us. Our hearts are not double. We pray for peace with your white children. So have they all said, your children of the plains.

*Chiefs of the Piegans
and Bloods
80 nights after the birth
of the Medicine Calf*

The Moon-When-Geese-Return, the moon of birth, had become for the Black-Footed-People a time of death.

A Prayer for Peace
June 1870

"THERE IS every reason to believe," wrote the Helena *Herald* of March 30, 1870, "that the raid of Colonel Baker, in addition to ridding the Territory of the most murderous band of Indians in the country, has also had a very salutary effect on the other tribes of the Blackfeet Nation.

"There is a good prospect of future peace and security."

Prospects had always been fairest when the Moon-When-Geese-Return rose over the Ground-Of-Many-Gifts. It was the time of joy. The time of awakening, restless and sweet. The time when Cold-Maker drew back his hand and bitter breath. When the land softened and warmed. When gaunt ponies freshened and shed their shaggy winter coats. When fathers opened to sons the secrets of the hunt, soon to be proved on the great spring herds, swollen with new-born calves. The time of new life.

159

The cycle of centuries commencing once more its eternal round. Sun's world reborn.

But in 1870 the Moon-When-Geese-Return brought no joy, no warmth, no new life to the Black-Footed-People.

They were, reported General Alfred Sully, "in so bad a condition that they cannot move...so many were dying with smallpox. There are many women and children left with no means of sustaining life, and without the government will feed them they must die of starvation."

The Moon-When-Geese-Return, the moon of birth, had become for the Black-Footed-People a time of death.

And so it was, with the lodges, once so bright and proud, now drab and saddened, slumped beneath the burden of disease and death, that the chiefs of the Blackfeet Nation met in council to speak of the deaths of The-Heavy-Runner and his people, and to decide upon war or peace with the white children of the Great Father.

Rising-Head spoke for the elders:

"Yes, it is true they have killed our women who were with child, and our new-born children. But the infant who was dragged along the ground was not killed. Their bullets killed the young son and young daughter of the new warrior chief, and the old warrior chief of the council. The chief of the band and the warrior chief fell under their blows. The rank of the first and the valor of the second did not make them stop. They did not respect the hair turned white by the winters, nor the hair of the young who had still to be guided by their mothers' hands when they were outside their lodges. Their vengeance is terrible. I know this. They have struck to the heart. I know this. The spirit of destruction was upon them. Sun also smiled upon them from above.

"Yet how can I hate these our enemies? And why not? Because they have come to the aid of our chiefs. They

160

have given fear to our young ones, who ridiculed our authority, not even listening to the war chiefs. Yes, Chiefs, you know we had lost our power with them. According to them, each day the hatred of the whites against us piles up more. And yet, without the whites, where would we be? They are the ones who furnish us with arms by which we vanquish our enemies. If the name Piegan strikes terror among the Crees, Assiniboins, and Gros Ventres, we owe this to the power of those arms. Could we then take up arms against the whites? I do not think we could.

"Yes, peace, peace with the whites, this is what we need. And we must have it at any price. Our blood probably will be the price. I hope we will not all perish.

"Soon the buffalo will be no more. Then who will hold out to our nation the hand of life? The whites alone will help us. They have strong hearts. Let us end the fighting. Perhaps we can be friends forever.

"I have said this."

Father John Imoda, a Jesuit missionary who lived and worked among the tribes of the Blackfeet Nation, confirmed "this general desire to make a lasting peace with the whites."

Writing to General Sully of a council he attended on March 17, 1870, Father Imoda reported that Mountain-Chief "desires to make with them a good and lasting peace"; that Aissaka, chief of the Fried-Grease band, "desired that a lasting friendship should be established again"; that Boy-Chief wished "that the past be forgotten, and that a good peace be made with the whites"; that Stoacgis, chief of the Lame-Bull band, "will not talk bad, and desires to make peace"; and that White-Calf, Generous-Woman, Cut-Hand, and Big-Talk, "chiefs of different bands of Piegans, were also present and spoke, but theirs being a repetition of the preceding, I think that the above be enough to persuade you."

Sully was persuaded.

"I think from what Father Imoda says," he wrote Commissioner Parker on April 12, "and from what I have learned from other sources, that the Piegans are somewhat frightened at the lesson they got, and have no wish for any further movement of troops this spring, or any more such severe punishment."

Lieutenant Pease, agent to the Blackfeet, was less certain, though still optimistic.

"It is impossible for me or anyone else to say what the Indians will do," he wrote Sully in May. "I am satisfied, however, that the head men of the Blackfeet will do all in their power to deter the young men from hostilities. But as you are aware, General, the young bucks do just as they please and do not take the trouble to consult their chiefs."

He need not have worried.

In late June 1870, there appeared before General Alfred Sully an unusual emmissary from the Bloods and Piegans. He was Jean L'Heureux.

"This gentleman, who calls himself a priest," Sully reported on July 10, "has lived a number of years with the Blackfeet, but the Catholic priests here do not recognize him and say he is an imposter, who is not reliable. Yet, as he could not possibly have any object in giving me the information he brings, I communicate it to you, as he is in a position with these Indians whereby he is better able to judge in regard to their feelings and disposition than any other person."

L'Heureux, who was known by the Blackfeet as Three-Persons, for his belief that the Great Spirit embodied three separate beings, Father, Son, and Holy Ghost, told Sully "that the Indians who escaped from the attack of the troops last winter suffered terribly in loss of

162

life...that a very large number of the squaws and children died on the way, from the severe cold weather and from smallpox."

The news confirmed Sully's growing conviction that "the great calamities which have lately visited this nation will tend to subdue them and cause them to beg for peace."

In further support of that conviction he forwarded to Washington the document which L'Heureux had brought him from the assembled chiefs of the Bloods and Piegans:

Country Of The People
Of The Plains
80 Nights After The Birth
Of the Medicine Calf

To Our Father On The Prickly Pear Prairie.

Your children, the People of the Plains, Bloods and Piegans, give you the hand of salutation.

The Three-Persons will go to your lodge. He will give news to you that our will is all good. He will discover to you our way of living, that you will have learned as well.

We made two large councils, the Bloods one and the Piegans one also. Your white children and us, we were looking into the way to live in peace.

Father, Three-Persons entirely heard the words of your children the chiefs, Bloods and Piegans. He will give you our wish for peace. Believe him.

Father, pity us. Discover now to us all your will. Cover the blood that was shed on the earth. Do not hate us. Our hearts are not double. We pray for peace with your white children.

So have they all said, your children of the plains.

Eagle-Tail-Raised, Bull-Back-Fat, Mountain-Chief, Many-Spotted-Horses, Calf-Coat, Medicine-Calf, Big-Feather, Black-Bear, and The-Lake, signed for the Bloods; Cut-Hand, Mountain-Chief, Rising-Head, Child-Calf, The-Crow-Woman, Many-Horses, Pole-Chief, The-Under-Bull, and Big-Lake, signed for the Piegans.

It was done. Two decades of warfare lay ahead on the plains. Not until 1891 would the last of the Sioux succumb at Wounded Knee. But Sioux and Cheyenne, Apache and Comanche would fight without their brothers of the Black-feet Nation. Never again would the Black-Footed-People, most favored of Sun's children, proud warriors of the northern plains, defend with arms the Ground-Of-Many-Gifts.

ABOUT THE ARTIST

Tom Saubert is more than a nationally exhibited, award-winning painter and sculptor. He's a Montanan. "To say anything about my work," he explains, "I must talk about Montana. The sounds and smells, the vast distances. The past and the present. It's home. The history, the land, and the people all possess a special wonderment for me that moves my spirit and sparks my imagination." Tom Saubert's unique feelings and talents combined to produce the remarkable drawings which illustrate and illumine *Death, Too, For The-Heavy-Runner.*

Bibliography

National Archives, Washington, D.C.

Letters Received, Office of Indian Affairs: a. Blackfeet Agency (1855-1869) b. Montana Superintendency (1864-1880).
Field Papers, Office of Indian Affairs: Montana Superintendency (1869-1873).

Montana Historical Society Library

Bonney, Orrin H. and Lorraine. *Battle Drums & Geysers.* The Swallow Press, 1970.
Ege, . R.J. *Strike Them Hard.* Old Army Press, 1970.
Post, Marie Caroline. *Life and Memoirs of General deTrobriand, USA.* E.P. Dutton, 1910.
Sharp, Paul F. *Whoop-Up Country.* University of Oklahoma Press, 1973.
deTrobriand, Regis. *Military Life in Dakota.* Alvord Memorial Commission, 1951.
Winners of the West. December, 1923 to December, 1944. No. 160, Microfilm, 2 rolls.
Selected Correspondence of the Montana Superintendency of the Bureau of Indian Affairs, 1869-1880. No. 75, Microfilm, 3 rolls.
Letters from Fort Ellis, October 24, 1869-July 14, 1876. No. 123, Microfilm, 1 roll.
U.S. Senate, Claims of the Heirs of Chief Heavy Runner. No. 53, Microfilm, 1 roll.
Letters, General Regis deTrobriand to members of his family, December 31, 1869 to November 6, 1871. Translated by Caroline M. Brammer. Owned by the Charles Post family.

167

Letters, Orders and Correspondence of General Regis deTrobriand, 1869-1870. SC 5, Montana Historical Society Archives.

Record of Engagements, Military Division of the Missouri, 1868-1882. Chicago, 1882. Compiled from Official Records.

U.S. Senate, Executive Document No. 49. *Message From President on Piegan Engagement.* 41st Congress, 2nd Session, February 19, 1870.

U.S. House of Representatives, Executive Document No. 185. *Letter from Secretary of the Interior on Expedition Against the Piegan Indians.* 41st Congress, 2nd Session, March 7, 1870.

U.S. House of Representatives, Executive Document No. 197. *Letter from Secretary of War on Expedition Against the Piegan Indians.* 41st Congress, 2nd Session, March 14, 1870.

U.S. House of Representatives, Executive Document No. 269. *Letter from Secretary of War Regarding Piegan Indians.* 41st Congress, 2nd Session, April 20, 1870.

U.S. House of Representatives. *Report of the Secretary of War.* 41st Congress, 2nd Session, November 20, 1869. (Volume 1: Hancock's Report: October 20, 1869).

U.S. House of Representatives, Executive Document No. 1, Part 3. *Report of the Secretary of the Interior.* 41st Congress, 2nd Session, November 15, 1869.

U.S. House of Representatives, Executive Document No. 1, Part 3. *Report of Commissioner of Indian Affairs.* 41st Congress, 2nd Session. December 23. 1869.

Ponsford, J.W. "Account of the Baker Battle." 1910 (Handwritten).

Noyes, A.J. Interview with Colonel S.C. Ashby. 1915 (Typewritten).

Plains Indian Museum

Letters Received by the Office of Indian Affairs, 1824-1881. Montana Superintendency, 1864-1880. National Archives Microfilm, Copy 234, Roll 490.

Letters Received by the Office of Indian Affairs, 1824-1881. Blackfeet Agency, 1855-1869. National Archives Microfilm, Copy 234, Roll 30.

Montana State University, Special Collections

The Baker Massacre. Told by Mrs. Agnes Embody of Valier, Montana to Mrs. Louis Floerschinger.

Newspapers

Montana: *Deer Lodge Independent; Helena Daily Herald; Helena Weekly Herald; Montana Post; New North-West; Rocky Mountain Gazette*
Chicago Tribune
New York Tribune
Washington Evening Star.

Published Works on Blackfeet Indians

Dempsey, Hugh A. *Crowfoot: Chief of the Blackfeet.* University of Oklahoma Press, 1972.

Ewers, John C. *The Blackfeet, Raiders of the Northwestern Plains.* University of Oklahoma Press, 1958.

—————————. *Indian Life on the Upper Missouri.* University of Oklahoma Press, 1968.
Grinnell, George Bird, *Blackfoot Lodge Tales,* University of Nebraska Press, 1962.
Lancaster, Richard. *Piegan.* Doubleday, 1966.
Schultz, James Willard. *Blackfeet and Buffalo: Memories of Life Among the Indians.* University of Oklahoma Press, 1962.

Published Works on Indians

Andrist, Ralph K. *The Last Death.* MacMillan Co., 1964.
Debo, Angie. *A History of the Indians of the United States.* University of Oklahoma Press, 1970.

Published Works on General William T. Sherman
Athearn, Robert G. *William Tecumseh Sherman and The Settlement of the West.* University of Oklahoma Press, 1956.
Hitchcock, Henry. *Marching With Sherman.* Yale University Press, 1927.
Lewis, Lloyd. *Sherman, Fighting Prophet.* Harcourt, Brace & Co., 1932.
Sherman, William T. *Memoirs.* New York, 1875.

Published Works on General Philip H. Sheridan

Hergesheimer, Joseph. *Philip H. Sheridan.* Houghton-Mifflin, 1931.
O'Connor, Richard. *Sheridan the Inevitable.* The Bobbs-Merrill Co., 1953.

Rister, Carl *Border Command — General Phil Sheridan in the West.*
University of Oklahoma Press, 1944.
Sheridan, Philip H. *Memoirs.* Charles L. Webster, 1888.

Background on Alfred Sully

Cullum, Bvt. Maj. Gen. George W. *Biographical Register of Officers
and Graduates of West Point.* Riverside Press, 1891.
Barsness, John and Dickinson, William. "Cannoneer's Hop,"
Montana Magazine, Summer, 1966.
Kingsbury, Lt. David L. "Sully's Expedition Against the Sioux,"
Minnesota Historical Society, VIII, 1923.
Sully, Langdon. "General Sully Reports." *American Heritage,* Vol.
XVI, No. 1, December, 1964.
White, Lonnie J. "Sully's Expedition to the North Canadian," *Journal
of the West,* Vol. XI, No. 1, January, 1972.
Wright, Robert M. "Reminiscences of Dodge," *Kansas State Histori-
cal Society Transactions,* 1905-1906.
Letters of Alfred Sully to Pennsylvania State Historian, July 2, 1872.
Personal correspondence with Langdon Sully, May through July,
1973.